BEST

Life-ing

HOW TO OVERCOME LIMITING BELIEFS, LIVE YOUR DREAMS AND CREATE FULFILMENT IN THE 7 AREAS OF LIFE—WITH OR WITHOUT THE "LIKES"

JULIA BRODSKA

DISCLAIMER

This is a work of creative nonfiction. The events are portrayed to the best of the author's memory. While all the stories in this book are true, some names and identifying details have been changed, in some cases the author has compressed events and in others she has made two people into one, to protect the privacy of the people involved.

BEST
Life-ing

Are you feeling stuck in life? Our online courses are for anyone who has unsuccessfully attempted to improve their overall health. It is designed so that you can go at your own pace. With a team of 20+ healers, teachers, and coaches, Best Life-ing can help you to achieve your dreams and fireach fulfilment in the 7 Areas of Life.

Reach out at www.bestlifeing.com, call us at (727) 777-LIFE, or contact Julia directly at julia@bestlifeing.com!

GRATITUDE

To my strong and talented mother, I love you with all my heart and you did an amazing job on your own. You ARE an inspiration and strength! I am eternally sorry for how much harder I made it for you in my teenage years and hope to be an adult you are proud to call your daughter.

To my dad, you are in my heart forever, and I miss you every day. I hope to make you proud. Thank you for your guidance.

To Bernard Kelly, thank you for believing in me and inspiring me to change my life. Your support has been endless and I am grateful to call you my friend and mentor.

TABLE OF CONTENTS

Introduction

WHAT DOES YOUR
BEST LIFE LOOK LIKE?

I magine the feeling of waking up every morning, knowing you're exactly where you belong. The place where you've always wanted to be, surrounded by everything you could have ever asked for. Think about yourself feeling complete at your core and confident in your life's purpose.

A life where you have meaningful relationships and friendships that you treasure, exciting new experiences often and a career that you are passionate about, pays well and makes an impact on the world.

Imagine the sense that nothing is ever missing, and even when things go seemingly wrong, you are in control. Imagine you are completely and entirely fulfilled. Fulfilled in yourself, in every desire and in each area that you have ever wanted to accomplish something.

Your life is everything that you have endlessly dreamed of and beyond what you imagined was possible.

While having your dream life may seem out of reach, it's no secret that people are doing it. And it's never too late or early. Envisioning, creating and achieving your best life will be the greatest thing you ever do.

1

This life is truly possible. And in this book, I will give you the belief that you can achieve it, the resilience to fight for your dreams and practical Action Steps to help you build momentum and confidence on your own unique journey.

HOW DO YOU DEFINE BEST LIFE-ING?

It is important to break down some of the terminology here first, because your thoughts and what you say to yourself are what creates your reality, regardless of whether your thoughts are deliberate or accidental. Here is why I propose that we refer to it as Best Life-ing:

According to the English Oxford Dictionary, the word best is primarily defined as "the most excellent, effective or desirable type or quality."

The word life regarding one's self is "the period between birth and death of a living thing."

Together when used in its context, if read literally, it sounds like a destination that we aspire to get to, without assuming entire control. This is important because of how your subconscious mind receives the message: "the most effective or desirable quality of the period between birth and death."

When we say, "living my best life," the verb "living" means "to spend one's life in a particular way or under particular circumstances"—the problem with this terminology is that it sounds as though there is no choice there; it sounds as though some of us are lucky and others wish we were there; again, your subconscious mind will receive this.

Hence, why I like to call it Best Life-ing, because the suffix "ing" denotes a verbal action, an instance of this or its results'. In other words, it is deliberate and intentional. I have found that there is a powerful importance in the way we talk to ourselves—the manner in which you speak to yourself and the words you choose, have an indisputable significance and direct impact on the results you achieve.

WHAT YOU'LL LEARN IN THIS BOOK

In the pages of this book, I will share with you my story: from being born in a war-torn country, to growing up in poverty and not being a native English speaker, to pushing past all these struggles to start two successful businesses, travel the world and teach Best Life-ing to small groups of 30 and auditoriums of over 900 corporate employees.

Each chapter of this book begins with a personal story from my life and then shares the lessons I learned and guiding principles that have led to my transformation from poverty to wealth, and from hopelessness to happiness. I call this process Best Life-ing.

Regardless of who you are, what you have and where you've been, you, too, can start Best Life-ing. If you're uncertain about being ready, don't worry. I was once just like you. But trust me. You just need to take one small step and your journey will begin, because small steps done consistently lead to massive action. This book is your first step. Every day you don't choose Best Life-ing, you cheat yourself out of life's amazing possibilities. You push your dream life further away.

Life is all about the questions we ask. I want to share my story, because with every mistake and difficulty there was a lesson. The lessons caused me to ask questions, and the answers changed my life. Every mistake leads to today. You are not alone in your experiences. You can learn and be inspired from others, just like I have.

I attribute everything that I've achieved to my not-so-desirable experiences. These experiences revealed what was missing in my life and sparked a desperate need to change. I did this by creating fulfilment in the seven areas of life. In this book, I will explain these areas in detail and teach you powerful strategies to master them. The seven areas of life are:

1. Relational

2. Intellectual

3. Spiritual

4. Vocational

5. Social

6. Physical

7. Financial

WHY I WROTE THIS BOOK

Why do I want to do this and help you find what I have found? Simple. Because someone once did it for me. And if they hadn't, I don't know where I would be today. I went from hating my life to passionately living my dreams! You can do the same. And you can do it much sooner than you think.

I couldn't have done it without the remarkable people that showed me how. My mentors and friends, as well as the many authors and industry experts who inspired and stretched my mind to unlock my potential. These teachers also taught me that successful people are not selfish. Serving others is the most fulfilling thing one can do, in whichever way we choose to do it. And there is no greater fulfillment than to find what you love, master it and then share it in service of others.

I have tremendous respect for you, the person willing to transform their life. It's scary and uncertain. You're sacrificing the lifestyle you know to fulfil your dreams. My passion and purpose is to help you succeed.

THE JOURNEY TO YOUR BEST LIFE BEGINS TODAY

By the end of this book, you will have all of the tools and components that are required for Best Life-ing. Best Life-ing is a holistic, enriching system that addresses your fulfilment in the seven areas of life. Master the individual elements, and you will tap into your inner strength to virtually limitless opportunities. This book is your blueprint for creating a truly fulfilled life in all areas.

By applying the methods in this book, you will identify your current fulfilment level in the seven areas of life, and understand why you are there. You will know how to decide what you want and make quicker decisions that are aligned with your goals. This will help you reduce needless complexity out of your life, identify and remove distractions, and create a plan for transformation that awakens your spirit and gives you a whole new perspective on living.

Don't find yourself being someone who lives a "fake great life" on the exterior (especially on social media) while being broken and unfulfilled inside. Take action to align your goals with your real life so that it becomes the one you've always dreamed of…with or without the "likes."

If you want to learn how to do that, then this book is for you.

If you feel like there are areas in your life that could be improved or the whole thing is just one big mess (like I did), then this book is for you. Let's do it!

Let's unleash your creativity, find your passion, build the right friendships or relationships you yearn for. Start that business, lose or gain the weight, get financial freedom and fall in love with life.

It isn't enough to just be here and exist. If you feel that life has got to be better than what it is right now, you're right. That's exactly where I was five years ago. I was $30,000 dollars in debt, overweight, uninspired in my career and just generally miserable. My life was going nowhere, until one night I realized I could no longer live with my unhappiness....

Prologue

ROCK BOTTOM

Have you ever woken up in the morning with a deep feeling that everything was just wrong? Even after trying to distract yourself and exhausting all of your positive-thinking methods, the feeling would still linger somewhere within your soul, right?

You might even think that this is just simply how your life is, or that life is just meant to be a grind. If I know one thing for sure, it is this: you are not alone. But it's truly incredible how a single moment that seemingly has no significance while you're in it, can change you forever.

I woke up one morning with a deep sense of emptiness and the feeling that every part of my life was a complete mess. Come to think about it now, I was waking up every morning with this feeling for a long time. I just did not notice it, because I became an expert in distracting myself from the unwanted emotions that I was feeling.

I finally got out of bed, had a shower, put my clothes on and reluctantly got in the car to drive to work. As if on autopilot, I put the radio on and blocked out the feeling inside of me. Today was just another mediocre day that had to happen before I had nothing else to do—when my days off finally came around.

I'd spend the rest of the day focusing upon something else: scrolling through Facebook, blaring loud music in my car or phoning a friend to complain about something. At work, my mindset was: *what do I need to do today to convince myself that I had done enough work and could justify that it was time to go home.*

As soon as I got in my car to leave the office, my only thought would be, *"Who could I go have dinner with tonight?"* Not so that I can enjoy their company or have a good meal, but ultimately so I could justify drinking wine—and a lot of it. This was my life Monday to Thursday; from Friday to Sunday that was a whole different story.

A NIGHT THAT CHANGED MY LIFE

On this night I decided to call Bernard. Bernard was my boss, my friend and in many ways my mentor. Bernard was a boss who was always good to me; he gave me his trust and pretty much let me do what I do.

Bernard as a friend was always supportive of me and my sometimes-crazy self. Bernard as a mentor always gave me the right advice. I was lucky to have such a close friendship with a person like him; I would hate to imagine how bad my life would have been if he was not a part of it at that time. Looking back now, I don't know how he had the patience to deal with me.

We had dinner and drank wine near my apartment, which was the norm; not because the food was that great, but because I was purely too lazy to go anywhere else. During dinner I spent the whole time trying to not talk about anything that would come anywhere near "deep and meaningful"— that would be simply too hard to deal with at the time.

From dinner we wandered back to my apartment, and I plopped myself on the couch and poured another wine. Wrapped in a white woolen blanket, I sat with the heater blazing on my feet. I would usually continue to drink and talk about anything until the wine would do its job and get me sleepy. Bernard would then say his farewells and head home—this wine, dine, sedate routine happened more times than I could possibly remember.

This night was pretty much like every other, except the wine wasn't doing its job and I couldn't shake off the chronic feeling that everything was wrong. It was the deep, sad feeling running through my body all day and, with my now clouded judgement, it could not be held in for even one more second.

I started crying. Not just a tear or two, but the full-blown wailing out loud. You know that really ugly, uncontrollable type of crying? That was me. I sobbed, feeling broken and unworthy about the state of my life.

"What is wrong, Julia?" Bernard asked as a look of surprise began to emerge on his face.

It wasn't that he didn't know how to respond. On the contrary, there was a slight satisfaction in his expression, like he had been waiting a long time for this breakdown to arrive, and now it was finally here.

"This is not where I wanted to be at the age of 27 years old!"

"What do you mean?" Bernard asked, still puzzled as to how the conversation had transpired to this.

Only moments earlier, I had spent the entire night staying off any real emotional subjects. After all, deep down inside I knew that my self-destructive lifestyle and behavior were the cause of my misery, even though I wasn't ready or willing to admit it.

"I'm overweight, I don't fit in any of my clothes anymore, and I can't afford new clothes. I am tired of my job, I have been doing pretty much the same thing my whole working life. It's not that I hate it, but I have just lost the passion, and I'm tired of doing the same thing over and over. I'm in so much debt! The banks keep calling me, and to be honest I have nothing to pay them with." I continued as a tidal wave of pent up emotions flooded out of me.

"I can never do anything to please my mom. I love my mom, but it just seems nothing I say and nothing I do can ever make her happy, let alone proud of me. I'm over my friends. That's if I can really even call them friends. I really love them, but I have started to notice over and over again that they aren't there for me when I need them, and they only call when it's time to party. Everything is always going a million miles an hour. I'm so tired, and even on my days off I never feel like I have had any rest. The only thing that used to relax me was yoga, but now I can't even afford that anymore! And I can't really change any of it, because I don't know how. Sometimes I think that I'm just not smart enough to ever make it in life."

There it was. The moment I finally accepted and admitted that I wasn't where I wanted to be. This is the first step in any form of successful change.

Even when I was sitting there with these things uncontrollably pouring out of my mouth, it was very clear that I felt like nothing was working out for me. Like many people I knew, I had created a false perception of where my life "should" be.

I had no idea how I had gained so much weight out of nowhere, but what made this worse was how terrible I felt inside; I had no energy and making change felt impossible. I truly believed I wasn't strong enough, and every time I caught a glimpse of myself in a mirror, I felt ashamed of who I had become.

Beyond this, I was deeply unfulfilled in my job. I had spent my whole working life building a career and climbing up the corporate ladder in business operations for a large company, you may have heard of it—McDonald's. There were many joyful and exciting moments, but the feeling of inspiration or challenge didn't exist anymore. And in my current victim state of mind, I couldn't see the benefits that all of this knowledge could and later would bring me. My only focus was that with all this debt to pay back, I was permanently stuck in my job and could never move forward with my life.

Speaking of which, I had over $30,000 worth of debt (not including my car loan). Just think about that for a moment—$30,000 debt and simply nothing to show for it! This personal financial crisis was created by living a lifestyle that I couldn't afford for over a decade.

I would build up debt, then make it the center of my attention, using most of my paycheck to pay some of it back. This pattern continued for years. I would rack up huge credit card bills without a care in the world; then I'd have a moment of panic and again try to repay it. But each time I built the debt back up, it became just that little bit harder to pay back, until eventually I just stopped caring. Before I knew it, I had let $5,000 turn into $10,000. And as the debt continued to snowball, I finally realized that I had a big problem—with everything combined, I owed more than half my annual salary before interest. Shit.

My priorities revolved around what people thought of me, and I measured my success by the material possessions I had gathered over the years. Outrageous amounts of money on clothes, designer bags, shoes, eating out and partying were dropped daily, without really contemplating how it would be paid back. These objects seemed so important to me at that time that I would have given anything to attain them.

My mom and I argued often about anything and everything; she had a good idea of the financial situation I was in (because I often called to borrow money), but she didn't quite know the magnitude of it. I didn't see her as frequently as I would have liked to, because it was easier to avoid these conversations at all costs.

I felt that many of my friends often let me down—I was fun to party with, but it usually didn't go deeper than that.

Constantly running around to every event I was invited to also took its toll on me. I never made time for myself or took a moment to think, knowing that if I did, I would be bombarded with my own thoughts and negativity.

When I was in a room with people smarter than me, I could hardly hold the conversation. I would get shy and extremely nervous because I felt self-conscious that I would be judged. This made me constantly think and believe that I would never achieve success myself, because I simply wasn't smart enough.

My emotional explosion slowed down, and the twenty minutes of dribble about how messed up my life was, was slowly coming to an end.

Bernard responded in a way that I will never forget...

"Julia, *you* have created this mess and *you* can also fix this mess if you really want to." He declared firmly, "If you want your life to be different, it is time to make some changes. These changes are not going to be easy and they are going to take some work."

The idea of more work wasn't exactly appealing at the time. After all, that's all that life felt to be—hard work. As I began to calm down, Bernard helped me realize that I had full control in the creation of my current life, and that I was very capable of creating the life I aspired to live, at any moment.

I knew Bernard was right. *It was time to make some changes and these changes were going to take work.* The vision of what this "work" would entail, felt as if it were a place so far away from where I was standing. I had no idea where to begin, and being so full of self doubt, it looked to be the longest road.

"Where do I start to fix my messed-up life, Bernard?" I felt defeated.

"Julia, there are many things I could suggest for you to do, but the only way you will really gain progress is if you start with doing the very basic things every single day," Bernard answered.

"Easy to say!" I responded.

"You need to read books to build your knowledge, and every day take 10 minutes for silence to clear your head and a 30 minute walk to improve your fitness." He simplified, "Cook your own food instead of eating out, to save some money and repay some of this debt."

"Bernard, I don't have enough time for all that," I interrupted.

"If you haven't got time for the basics, stop complaining about your messed-up life!" Bernard replied firmly in a tone I had not heard aimed at me before. This stopped the excuses and captured all of my attention.

TRANSFORMATION BEGINS WITH REFLECTION

Bernard's words were like a cold splash of water to the face. They snapped me out of what seemed like a trance, and sparked questions within me, "How did I get here? Was I ready to change? Could I really give up my current lifestyle, with only a *hope* that it could get better?"

Even though I could acknowledge it wasn't working, the fear that the grass might not be greener made it seem that I had a lot to lose.

What I didn't know then, was that action builds momentum, and momentum brings more action through self belief and empowerment. Accomplishment gives you a healthy hit of dopamine, which makes you want more. Soon, you begin to amaze even yourself—it's truly incredible what the human mind can push the body to achieve.

There was so much more to get out of my day and, ultimately, my life.

And on this evening, I was ready, I was able and I was determined to make a change.

But to do that I would first need to reflect on where I've been and where things went wrong. And that started when I was just a child, in a world and country far different than where I lived now...

Chapter One

HOW BELIEFS SHAPE YOUR LIFE
FOR SUCCESS OR FAILURE

LIMITING BELIEF FUNDAMENTALS

Ukraine was in its freezing winter of 1991. The streets were destroyed and grimy smoke poured from building windows, a result of the explosive shells and bullets that had pierced the glass. Tanks shared the main roads with people wounded from the newly acquired guns of the residents, enraged in their protests commanding Russians to get off their land.

Alla, a beautiful 32-year-old woman, sat in the kitchen of her second floor apartment on a main road in Odessa. She had lovely, long blonde hair with curls that flicked at the ends. Her eyes were blue and her skin light and unblemished.

Alla held a pan over five candles that were standing upright in a metal container to cook eggs for her two-year-old daughter. Suddenly, the sound of her newborn screaming from the other room unnerved her. As she glanced out from her window, a sharp wave of panic overcame her to see that the milk truck arrived at the grocer located directly below the apartment. She had come to know that by the time she made it down the stairs, a swarm of people would have cleaned out the truck in desperation from the lack of resources.

Alla was my mother, the newborn was my sister Nataliya and the two-year-old was me. There was no electricity or gas in our apartment, and the battle to keep warm was a constant struggle in the -24 °C temperature and with the sharp chill of the northeasterly winds. She picked us up, dressed us in on our coats, beanies, scarves and gloves, then prepared the stroller. She grabbed her keys from the dark wooden hallway table and proceeded out the door.

As she walked down the road to her workplace with her two small children, she begged God for safety. My mom had to collect her paycheck and find food.

Upon arriving at her workplace, my mom was told by her boss that Russian would no longer be the language in Ukraine and when she returned from maternity leave she would need to know the new Ukrainian language. Not knowing what was going to happen in the immediate or distant future, my mom wondered if she should learn Ukrainian or English instead.

MY STORY STARTED JUST 2 YEARS PRIOR

On February 15th, 1989, I was born in Odessa, Ukraine. My father, Michael, was a 44-year-old executive for a building company and my mother, Alla, was a 30-year-old accountant. They were crazy in love with each other and well established in their jobs and finances. My mom has always told me, their plan was to have as many kids as God would give them.

My parents had a wonderful life set up for us. They were hard workers, successful in their pursuits and incredibly kind, happy people. They loved my sister and I with all their hearts. They owned an apartment in Moscow, which we would spend the weekdays in, and a house in Odessa that was once my dad's dream to build with his own hands. We would drive or catch a European train to the house on the weekend. I imagine everything was perfect in those moments of their life, especially in comparison to what was about to come.

In 1989, the revolutions of the USSR occurred, which resulted in the end of the communist rule in Central and Eastern Europe. The period is sometimes referred to as the Autumn of Nations.

My sister Nataliya was soon born on February 4th, 1991. My parents were stressed with the war in the streets, constant murder and the decline of the financial economy. They needed and planned to change their lives. But time ran out. My dad had a stroke at the age of 47 and was diagnosed with dementia.

Dementia is a chronic and incurable disorder that deteriorates the brain. Over time it affects thinking, behavior and the ability to perform everyday tasks. When my mother was told there was no cure, she did not accept this. In 1993, my parents left everything behind and moved our lives to Sydney, Australia.

This move was incredibly hard for me, and I know my parents struggled immensely during this time. The years to come were particularly challenging for my mother, leaving her parents, other family and friends behind, and having no knowledge or understanding of the language and very little money. Worst of all, no one in Australia cared about her international accounting degree, which made it very difficult to find work. These were a few of the challenges and sacrifices that my mom had to make for our family. She recalls it as the most traumatic time of her life.

My mom had a four-year-old (me) and my two-year-old sister to look after on her own, while the man of her dreams was rapidly also becoming a dependent. My mother is my hero. I hate to imagine her having to find the strength to get through this dark storm, but she didn't have a choice, so she had to find ways to cope and provide for all of us.

My mom began by getting work: cleaning people's houses for $50 a day. This wasn't a lot of money, but by working seven days a week, she would get enough to feed us and pay the rent. After work, my mom would go to night school to learn English. She did this for the next three years, before she had to restart her whole entire accounting degree, which took another five.

As a young kid, I observed my mother's struggle; I cared and wanted to help. I was only seven years old, but I knew we had no money because I was told so every time I whined for something.

One day we were at a community fair, and there was a magician busking in the middle of the closed down road. He was doing a magic trick in which he collected a gold coin from everyone. Whatever he was supposed to do didn't work out, and all of the coins came flying out of his hat all over the pavement. Without a second thought, I picked up as many of the coins as I could and I came running over to my mother with my handful and huge grin.

"Look mommy, I've got us some money," I said, having no understanding of its value or worth. She looked at me shocked and embarrassed.

"Julia!" she shouted in disappointment. "You cannot pick up something another has dropped and claim it as your own. Go back to the magician and tell him you have found his money that he lost."

Confused and deflated, I walked back to the magician and returned his hard earned money. This made me feel like there was nothing I could do to help. Seeing my mother so upset and disappointed, I felt that I had really let her down. I only ever wanted to make my mother proud, but this was going to be the first of many disappointments.

Though my understanding of my mother's financial struggle was already evident to me, it became more significant when I started school.

MY FIRST DAY OF SCHOOL IN A FOREIGN COUNTRY

My first day in primary school was a hot Sydney summer day in February. My mother couldn't afford a proper uniform at that moment, so the school allowed me to wear a yellow polo shirt and blue shorts. These colors matched the school's uniform colors, except everyone else had a logo on their shirts. As I walked into the kindergarten classroom, instantly every other kid pointed at me. I didn't know why because I couldn't speak or understand English, so I walked in and sat down in this frightening room.

The teacher tried to introduce me using gestures and facial expressions to another girl sitting across the room. Maria was Russian also and she translated that the teacher wanted me to move and sit next to her.

Maria was very nice to me and became my first friend in Australia. She made my life a little more pleasant, but all I really wanted to do was go back home to Russia. At recess, other kids approached me and tried speaking to me, but I simply couldn't understand. They began pointing and laughing at me.

"What are they saying to me?" I asked Maria in Russian.

"They are calling you a boy," she translated. I could hear the deep shame in her voice.

"Why are they calling me a boy? I'm not a boy," I asked, confused and feeling a little wounded.

"It's because you are wearing shorts," she explained. "And that's what all the boys do."

This moment became the start of my tormenting primary school years and a significant component to the many limiting beliefs that I later would create.

My first English word was "stupid" because that's what the kids called me at school.

LIFE AT HOME

"I want to go home to Russia, why did you bring me here?" Each and every night for the first year of being in Australia, at exactly dinner time I would cry and scream this to my mom.

Every morning I would then wake up, arrive at school and pretend everything was okay. This was the destructive mind-training that I was unknowingly putting myself through many years later, when I felt it was more important to pretend to be happy, rather than actually being it.

Somehow my mom managed to make sure my sister and I never went without, and did everything she could to give us the best chance at life. She soon enrolled us into extracurricular activities like swimming, dancing and tennis. She wanted us to develop our skills, make new friends and to help us find what we enjoyed.

My mom believes that having an education is crucial to success in life, therefore tutoring and homework was a compulsory daily task.

Back then I hated the strict routine we lived by every day, but I mostly did what I was told. On the weekends, I frequently threw tantrums because I wasn't allowed to play outside with the other kids who lived in the neighborhood until I had finished my bookwork. Their distracting laughter made it hard to focus. And usually by the time I finished, it was time for them to go home.

In year three, we moved to a Sydney suburb by the beach called Coogee. I left the school I was at and moved to a new one in the new area. By this stage I hated school. I was picked on for being different, and my English still wasn't strong. I had only one friend, Maria, who I now had to leave behind.

The adults around me would say, "Don't worry, this is your chance to start fresh" and "Everything is going to be okay."

So the thought crossed my mind, *"Maybe people will like me at my new school, maybe I will make some friends."* No, fate had other plans. There was no escaping this great lesson.

I walked in on my first day into Mr. Kell's class. He introduced me to the room, but I could barely say hello. My confidence was very broken by this point. My English had improved somewhat but it was obvious that I couldn't speak like the other kids, which in their opinion made me "stupid."

After the introduction, Mr. Kell said, "Who would like to sit next to our new student?"

The room remained silent, which didn't surprise me. But still. It felt like the longest and loudest silence, until suddenly...

"She can sit next to me," I heard as I looked up at a tall, ashy blonde kid sitting at the head of a six-seater square table. His name was Simon.

Simon and I became great friends growing up. He was always kind to me, but my biggest concern was that I didn't want him to become a "loser" because of me. The kids frequently called me a loser, so despite not liking it, that's what I believed I was.

This is one of the amazing abilities of our minds; they are so skilled at creating beliefs based on popular consensus and information that we are told repeatedly, that it has a way of convincing, not only others, but also ourselves that those things are the truth.

Simon was never ashamed of me. He had so much wisdom and purity about his soul. He was humble and considerate, and I am forever grateful that he unknowingly helped me as best he could during those days.

MY FATHER'S PROGRESSING ILLNESS AND ITS TOLL ON MY FAMILY

In the last of my primary school years, my father was deteriorating badly. He couldn't walk or speak properly anymore, which gave the other kids at school even more opportunity to make fun of me for this misfortune.

Back then I didn't understand. I was embarrassed and even ashamed of him dropping me off and picking me up from school. I would decline the offer every morning and beg him to let my sister and I walk alone. Sometimes I went to the pathetic extremes of running out of school first or early so that my dad wasn't seen waiting for me at the gate, just to avoid hearing "your dad's a retard" from the other kids.

I look back at those days with pure regret, for missing the only chances that I had to get to know my dad. I rejected and wasted those precious opportunities because I allowed other people's words and opinions to get to me and, in turn, control my actions.

One day, my dad fell down the stairs while we were at school. Luckily, our neighbors called the ambulance and he was safely taken to the hospital. But once there, my family was hit with some bad news. The doctors identified that he was now paralyzed from the fall. And since my mother was unable to provide full-time care or the living conditions required for a wheelchair, she had to admit her husband into a nursing home. I stop and think sometimes today how that would feel.

Many people spend so much time and energy searching for the man or woman of their dreams. My parents found this, but five short years later, this became their "ever after." Their marriage once bright and full of promise, now seemed bleak and hopeless. How could they move forward happily? The doctor's diagnosis of my father and the subsequent move to the nursing home that followed seemed like a death sentence. The situation felt completely life shattering.

For another three years, my mother traveled an hour from home to work, still cleaning people's houses for $50 cash per day, then to the nursing home another hour away by bus, then home to feed the kids and then night school to finish her studies. Life was a marathon for her. And looking back now, I could imagine how hard, uninspiring and difficult this would have been.

She would always say, "I have to do it for my kids." Her prayers continuously filled with fear, "Please God, don't let anything happen to me until they are old enough to fend for themselves."

My sister and I would do the occasional visit to the nursing home when my mother forced us to, but I had grown so distant from my dad, as he was deteriorating so severely at this stage. He didn't remember us, and he couldn't recognize who we were. This hurt me deeply.

He often became violent, disoriented and so incredibly lost. I hated seeing him like this. It is a very painful feeling when your dad doesn't know who you are and, worse, you don't know who he is either.

I didn't entirely recognize the magnitude of what was going on, the consequences and regrets that would one day follow. I devotedly shunned anything that would trigger the feelings—I became good at blocking pain out of my mind and life, but I also became cold and resentful.

Lessons

THE POWER OF BELIEFS

Before we get into the seven areas of life, it's important for us to discuss a topic that underpins each area and everything you'll learn in this book: belief.

One of the biggest lies we humans choose to accept is that our beliefs are facts. We all want to think our opinions, convictions and views accurately reflect reality. That what we believe in is true. No one likes to be wrong.

Our beliefs greatly influence our emotions and actions, and we use them to understand and navigate the world. Many researchers would agree that the majority or our core and fundamental beliefs are formed by the age of six. Generally, these beliefs are formed in two ways: through our own experiences and by accepting what others tell us to be true.

Once formed, our beliefs become embedded in us. And they play a critical role in shaping the direction of our lives. Regardless of whether they are actually true or not, we live as if they are factual. Our beliefs determine if we consider something to be good or bad, right or wrong, beautiful or ugly, safe or dangerous, or acceptable or unacceptable. Beliefs influence our decisions—whether we choose to follow our dreams or accept mediocrity, complain or take action, hit the gym or spend the evening on the couch. Beliefs matter.

But how can we give so much credit to something that by its very definition is not a fact? If we look at the dictionary definition, nowhere will you find the word "fact." Instead, it is defined as:

An acceptance that a statement is true or that something exists. A firmly held opinion or conviction.

Even if multiple people agree on it, a belief is only a thought in the mind that we have thought long enough to the point where we accept it as true. There is no need to be attached to any of them or be convinced they are truth. We don't even need to accept them, especially those that don't serve us. You are as capable as you want to be. You are as worthy as you think.

So often we pass up potential opportunities because we allow the mind to tell us we "can't." This is your conscious mind operating on fears developed from past experiences and other people's belief systems. Once an idea or a thought enters your mind, you only have a few seconds to act on it before the conscious mind talks you out of it with excuses like: *I can't afford it, I'm not smart enough, the industry has too much competition and so on. Before you know it, the idea is out of reach, according to your mind.*

The great news is, it's completely in your control and you need ZERO resources to change the thoughts you choose to think. Ignore your conscious mind (the one you can hear) to tap into your subconscious mind (the creative workspace that is constantly drowned out by all the noise) by practicing silence. Stop concerning yourself with all the details. Take some sort of action to immediately get you going, and the answers you need will come when you need them. Your subconscious mind already has all the answers. You just need to believe in yourself and the possibilities.

DO YOUR LABELS DEFINE YOU?

We often identify with labels to describe who we are. Unfortunately, in many cases these labels limit us. Labels categorize our personalities based on the work we do, our hobbies and our behaviors. We are not our labels, but often we choose to identify with them and believe they are true.

For example, although I didn't like that I was called "stupid" as a child, I would subconsciously believe that it was true. And this held me back from achieving many things.

The victim mentality was something I lived with for a long time. I believed I wasn't able to do certain things, because "bad things always happened to me." Victim is just another label. And regardless of our circumstances, we do not need to live it and wear it. Instead, you can identify your self-created, negative labels and use them as a source of motivation to rewrite them and positively change your self-image.

It is completely unnecessary to identify with any label, even if an event or circumstance has given you validity to do so. You are not your labels. Your soul is pure. It is, however, the mind that wants labels. Labels help our minds feel comfortable in an uncertain world. They help us feel like we "fit in" and justify our actions and experiences. With enough practice, you can teach your mind not to believe these labels by telling it what you *want* to identify with instead.

Regardless of what your beliefs are, the fact of the matter is that your beliefs are just that—beliefs, not facts. Understanding this can help you change your beliefs and achieve limitless potential. Do the Action Steps and apply the methods in this book. Don't skip any. Whatever you choose to believe, you are right. We create our own realities whether we do it deliberately or not.

By challenging my own beliefs of what I could and couldn't do, my ideas of what is right and wrong, and the level of importance that I placed on what other people said and thought, I learned how to find what I love and how to live what I believe.

We can challenge and change our beliefs as often as we desire because there is no need to get attached to them—they're just thoughts.

DO YOUR ACTIONS SUPPORT YOUR BELIEFS?

We have so many beliefs, yet there are many of us who are not living the beliefs that they so strongly believe. For example, I've met a person who believes "all rich people are evil and selfish" and another who swears that "money changes people." You probably won't be surprised to learn that both these people were not financially fulfilled.

I've met another person who believes veganism is extremely important for health, animal protection and the environment, yet his leather car seats and cashmere jackets don't seem to rattle him as much as what other people are ordering for lunch.

Matthew Kelly wrote a great book called *Perfectly Yourself*. A great quote that impacted my life from this book is: "The problem isn't that we don't believe, but rather we do not live what we believe."

Instead, our beliefs are typically all in the head—biases, judgemental thoughts and ideologies that sometimes unintentionally cause pain. We compare ourselves to others. We remind ourselves of what we "can't" do or what is impossible. We create excuses and justify our arguments for not chasing our dreams.

Stop wasting precious moments, because of yours or others' beliefs: even if you think you can't, give it a go anyway. Find the way to believe you *can*. What other people think is none of your business.

Choose what you believe; change it if you need to (and as often as you like). Make sure your beliefs serve you, and live what you believe.

NOW IT'S YOUR TURN

Take the time to observe your beliefs. What do you fight for? What are your limitations and the boundaries you set for yourself? What are your beliefs about money, love, happiness and success?

Once you have identified the beliefs that shape your perspective, ask yourself, "How do I know whether my beliefs are true? What evidence do I have to prove their accuracy? Do they support my dreams or hold me back? If they are of no benefit to you, stop believing them. Think the thoughts that propel you towards your best life, and eventually those will not only start to dominate your mind, but materialize in your real life.

Changing your own beliefs is easier than you may think. Identify a limiting belief that holds you back in life, then go to Google and research the opposite. You'll almost certainly find many facts and arguments that discredit what you think.

Diary Entry

March 7th, 2019 – Cairns, Australia

I AM LIMITLESS!

Petrified! The most accurate word to describe the feeling I felt as I was lowering my body into the Australian Great Barrier Reef. There's a certain level of discomfort in not being able to breathe easily. Though I have been alive for over thirty years and lived in Australia for most of them, I've never taken the time to see this incredible natural wonder of the world. This could possibly be my last opportunity. I needed to do it!

I am usually the person who is scared of things that cause adrenaline. In fact, I usually do everything I can to bring stillness into my world. Jumping out of planes, roller coasters and scuba diving aren't really my thing. However, limiting beliefs don't usually stop me anymore. My focus is to keep the "can'ts," "impossibles" and other limiting words out of my vocabulary. However, I do still have fears like everyone else. These waters challenged me, especially since this was my first time scuba diving and the potential consequences paralyzed me in fear. Aside from not being able to breathe properly, there were other risks. Coming up too fast, losing oxygen or encountering some of Australia's dangerous wildlife could prove fatal.

But I couldn't let those worries stop me.

It was time to get a grip or miss out! I'm not exactly sure if I can say I built up the courage to scuba dive, but I did do it anyway. And it was absolutely incredible: shimmering deep blue water with a seemingly silk flow, draped like curtains, sun rays beaming through the gaps of coral and textured stone, and the movement of the elegant residents welcoming us into their home.

The fear wore off. Stillness overtook my body and silenced my mind, as though the ocean was whispering that everything would be alright. I never wanted to leave.

Diving the Great Barrier Reef was an incredibly majestic experience. The fear that made me feel alive was also the reward.

Jumping into the bottom of the ocean was one of the most thrilling, yet therapeutic experiences. And fear makes us live in the present moment. By conquering it, we gain confidence and can take on bigger challenges while pushing past even bigger fears. Limiting beliefs may creep up every now and again, but isn't it natural to question ourselves? We just have to be careful not to let any beliefs limit us in this short life.

KEY POINTS:

1. There is no use in holding onto a belief that limits you. A belief is just a thought that you have thought about long enough to believe.

2. Do not allow yourself to take on or identify with the labels that people give you. Doing so smothers your growth and puts you in a box.

3. Don't waste precious moments, because you care what people think. I tried to impress people, fit in or not disappoint them to avoid being disliked or bullied. All this did was lengthen the time it took to realize my dreams.

4. You are not a victim. No matter what the conditions, you do not have to identify with this label.

5. Feel free to choose and change your beliefs whenever you want.

31

ACTION STEPS:

Think about and write down the following thoughts:

1. Write down your beliefs about time, love, money, family and success.

2. Which of these do you know to be true without a shadow of a doubt?

3. What labels are you wearing? I was dumb, poor and a victim. What labels would you rather have?

4. Brainstorm new beliefs for any negative labels you identified in Step One. Remember, these new beliefs don't need to be true just yet. For example, if you've believed "I'm always broke" for most of your life, thinking "I am capable of achieving financial freedom" isn't going to rocket you straight to riches. Instead, your new beliefs will serve as new thoughts that you will start to believe, which will eventually materialize in your life if you consistently believe in them.

Chapter Two

LONELY STREETS

AREA OF LIFE 1/7: RELATIONAL

June 1st, 2001, was a cold winter's night in Sydney. I was 12 years old, and my friend Shannon was sleeping over. It was around 1 a.m. when the home phone rang. I remember thinking it was very unusual because my mom had a very strict policy about phone calls after 9 p.m.

She was constantly reminding me that it was rude to disturb a household with phone calls during the sleeping hours between 9 p.m. and 9 a.m. None of my friends were allowed to call me, and I was not allowed to call them.

I hurried into her room to see who it was and call her out on being a hypocrite if it was one of her friends, or prepare to get yelled at if it were one of mine.

"Who was it?" I asked eagerly as she hung up the phone. She was silent for a moment.

"Shannon, I am sorry, but we need to call your mother to pick you up and take you home," my mother responded, completely ignoring my question.

"What! Why mom?" I yelled with instant rage. "You promised she could stay over!"

My mother repeated, "Shannon, please call your mother to pick you up."

Shannon looked at me disappointed and confused, while I looked back with fury. I had come to blame my parents for the cause of my unhappiness, even though they did everything they could to give my sister and I a wonderful life.

I was boiling with anger as we waited for Shannon's mother to pick her up. But my mother didn't say a word. I sat at the end of the lounge, wondering why my mom had made such a drastic decision; were we laughing too loud and making too much noise? Or maybe she was annoyed that we didn't clean the mess we left in the living room after playing Monopoly.

The silence was deafening, and minutes felt like hours as my mom sat quietly at the other end of the room. I kept probing her for answers, which soon turned to screaming and demanding; I wanted to know what we had done. My mom remained silent on the couch, ignoring my frenzy.

Finally, Shannon's mom arrived and they left. My mom then asked my sister and I to sit down and join her on the couch. Disobediently I sat on the floor. My mom's eyes began to fill with water, and as soon as that first tear broke free, her cry became an untamed river.

"That was the hospital. Your father has passed away tonight," she wept, placing both elbows on her knees and her head into her palms.

My heart sank. My mother's was broken. It felt like someone was squeezing my heart from inside and pushing down on my chest at the same time. Every breath felt hollow in my lungs, as if I was suffocating; the throbbing was so powerful it seemed there was no coming back.

At only 12 years old, I had no idea how to deal with a loss so great. For my mom's sake, I wish I could change what I did next. I stormed into my room and slammed the door shut. And with that, I shut the whole world out emotionally for the next decade.

I sat and cried all night. I didn't comfort my mother or sister and wanted nothing to do with the pain my family was feeling. It felt so unfair. I thought, *"All the other kids get two parents, why not me? Hasn't life tortured me enough?"* I was falling apart when my family needed me most.

From there it became a downward spiral. I came to the conclusion that no amount of action would change anything, and I convinced myself that I couldn't control what was going to happen in my life. Life was bullshit. I couldn't see any reason to put work or effort into anything long term. After all, I believed everything could flip on you at any second. So what was the point?

Inside the church at my dad's funeral, the small handful of people in attendance amplified the emptiness of every chair that should have been occupied by a relative or friend from Russia. Instead, the vacant seats served as a brutal reminder that, in the end, we are always alone. Black styled the room by those who could make it; their clothes and energies were accessories to the pale faces and puffy eyes they wore. I sat broken in the front row of the church, wishing everything was as dark and foggy as my emotions.

During the ceremony, I didn't hear a word that was said—all of my senses were exhausted of agony—it was just murmurs through my blocked ears, a salty taste on my wet lips and liquid drowning my eyes. The same endless throbbing pain from my heart was now pounding through all of my body.

Everything felt like it was in slow motion. I looked over at my mother, her face a perfect picture of controlled sadness, who was trying to stay strong for us. But the slow tears rolling down her cheeks gave away that she, too, was broken.

Watching my dad get buried was the worst thing I have ever seen. The sun shone radiantly above us; the sky's dazzling blue glare was offensively cheerful. It was as if God had conspired to make it known that life would continue along just fine without my dad.

I stared back at the inconsiderate sky, imagining how I could escape my life entirely. I longed for closure. But I detached from my emotions again, because facing them wouldn't be enough to erase my need for acceptance of my father's passing.

He was gone. The decision was final, and no amount of tears or pain would bring my dad back to this world. It was time to go home as a new family, smaller and tainted, with a little less hope.

My mom always used to tell me I had to get an education.

"Julia, you need to study and get good grades or you will end up like me cleaning toilets your whole life."

"Screw it, what good did it do for you?" I'd yell. "You studied and now no one gives a shit about it! You're back to studying in your 40s. What's the point?"—Imagine if your 12-year-old child spoke to you like that.

"Dad studied all his life, too. What good did his education do for him? He just had a stroke and suffered for nearly 10 years. He couldn't walk, talk, bathe himself or function, and then he died at 56. What's the point of wasting my time on getting an education? It did NOTHING for either of you!"

My poor, grieving mother was so broken, and I spent every waking moment making it more difficult for her. I had no consideration for what she was going through. I was full of hate and anger at the world. Now that my mother was the only adult figure of the household, I resented her, too.

In the weeks following my dad's funeral, I soon gave up all extracurricular activities, dropped out of weekend tutoring and refused to listen to pretty much anything my mom told me to do. Because I internally blamed her and sensed she was in a fragile state, I felt compelled to say "no" to everything that she asked of me—making it all the more difficult for her in this horrific time.

The next four years I put her through hell, and I am eternally sorry for how I continually hurt such an amazing, resilient woman. Here goes the dreadful part of my story that truly hurts me to remember and share.

THE YEARS AFTER MY DAD'S DEATH

Simon's father passed away around the same time as mine. He became my rock and the only person I felt I could truly open up to and talk deeply with about my emotions and life—he was the only one who really understood me.

High school started and we found out that we were going to the same new school. I was over the moon! Simon inspired my confidence in many ways but, unfortunately, I used that confidence to fuel all the wrong habits. Having experienced so much bullying in the past, I craved to be accepted and would do anything to not be different. I just wanted to "fit in."

During this period, Simon and I would only occasionally catch up in person. We both had newfound friends that we were spending more time with. So instead, we spoke on the phone more often, to stay up-to-date with each other's lives. Whenever something important happened, he was the first person I would call, and vice versa. Our friendship remained strong, even though we were not always together.

My antics with my new friends at school were not the type you'd want your daughter to be involved in. Despite my efforts, most of the other kids didn't like me very much in high school either—I wasn't confident around the assertive kids, and I found my place with the outcasts who didn't care much for life, success or results either.

In the first two years of high school, I was in the top classes, getting the second highest Math grades out of all sophomore students in the entire school. My tutoring was really paying off, as I was doing fairly well in all my other subjects. Too bad I didn't care for grades or success. Soon I started to skip class because I was bored and wanted to rebel. I felt that when I did something wrong, I punished the world, the same way the world had punished me.

Each morning on the bus, I would befriend anyone who was willing to skip school with me, and we would jump off half way at Maroubra beach to drink alcohol and smoke cigarettes. My main partner in crime was a girl named Alison. We bonded over our troubles and hatred of the world.

The problem with hate is that it pollutes your soul and imprisons your spirit. Poison isn't always something that needs to be consumed or injected into your body, and hate is a strong, poisonous emotion that eats you up inside and causes contagious destruction—it especially blossoms when you indulge and share it with others.

Alison and I would loiter in the streets, car parks and on the beach throughout the school hours and into the night. I cared very little about getting caught or the consequences. My powerless mother would be worried sick, but I would ignore her calls. Sometimes I would lie to keep the peace, but mostly I would respond with rude profanities to ensure she knew just how much I didn't care. Again, this was my way of punishing the world and everyone in it.

By 13, I had a filthy attitude towards all adults and life in general. I was so lost and angry, and the only way of release I knew was to project it out onto everyone else. It saddens me to think about how much I hated myself back then, but somewhere in the back of my mind, I wanted to do right and be a good person—I just had no idea what that looked like.

My thoughts were constantly dark, and I believed there was no point in trying to do a good job at anything. I convinced myself that there were no guarantees in life. In my perception even if I did everything right and worked hard, I could end up like my parents.

Your thoughts become your reality. You attract the people, places and experiences in your life based on the energy you put out and the thoughts you think all day. Whether your thoughts are intentional, accidental, good or bad, what you think about invites the world that you get. That's all you can get when it's what you're looking for and expecting. For example, I was once told a great story about two people in a mall. One was a married man, who loved working out at the gym, and the other was a single woman who enjoyed going out to bars. They strolled through the shopping center together one Friday afternoon window shopping. Neither of them were there to specifically buy anything, they were just catching up for a coffee. As they walked through the center to the cafe, the man noticed all of the activewear and sneakers while the woman noticed all of the nice heels and dresses in the windows. They were walking together, in the same place and at the same time, yet having a completely different experience. The man who loved the gym noticed items he could use while working out. And the woman who enjoyed the bars saw apparel she could wear on nights out. Their mindsets dictated their experiences.

LISA, DRUGS AND RUN-INS WITH THE LAW

Upon moving to Coogee, I met a girl next door named Lisa. Lisa was always fun to be around. And like me, she had gone through many difficulties at her age, which bonded us. She was only six months older, but I looked up to her; she was loud, outgoing, funny and confident, which made her the ringleader of her group—I intensely wanted to be like that.

Her father drank a copious amount of alcohol from the early hours of the morning. On a few occasions we witnessed him drink himself to the point where he had epileptic fit episodes. If you have ever seen this, you know that it is a horrific experience, particularly for a child to witness.

Lisa's aunt and older cousin, who she lived with, drank alcohol often and my memories of those days consisted of domestic arguments and fights, car accidents and regular DUIs.

We began to steal hard liquor from her dad, aunt and cousins' unlimited liquor cabinet to experiment and entertain ourselves. We drank it in the park to avoid being caught.

One day instead of going to school, we drank vodka in the park all day and into the late afternoon.

"Do you want to try smoking weed?" Lisa asked me.

"I don't know," I replied apprehensively.

"Don't worry, I've done it before…it feels nothing like alcohol. You won't be out of your mind or off your head. You will have fun and be very relaxed," she encouraged.

I really wanted Lisa to think I was cool, so I agreed and smoked marijuana for the first time. This was the first of many stupid and dangerous decisions that I made at that age, in the hopes of impressing her and my new group of friends.

Rejection is a form of identity destruction that many of us try to avoid because of the fear associated with not being accepted by our peers. We all want to belong and feel accepted for who we are, but there can be stages in our lives where we are unsure of exactly who that is. This causes us to seek approval from others and behave accordingly.

Eventually, I realized that if I misbehaved, people stopped calling me a "goody-goody," and they even congratulated me on my rebellious behavior, which made me want to rebel even more. For the first time in my life, people treated me like I was "cool" and "brave." I liked these labels so I pretended to be them.

It worked! I wasn't different anymore (well at least not a loser). According to my classmates, I was tough and a risk-taker. I started smoking weed and drinking almost every single day with anyone who wanted to cut school with me.

One afternoon, Lisa and I were sitting in the food court of a shopping center.

"Have you ever gone shopping with a five fingered discount?" Lisa whispered.

"What does that mean?" I asked.

"Five fingers…get it?" she said as she showed me her hand. I still didn't get it and looked confused.

"Shoplifting you idiot!" she exclaimed.

"Oh, no!" I whispered, knowing this was a bad idea.

"Let's do it!" she said excitedly. "It'll be fun!"

Lisa stood up from the table eagerly while I contemplated if it was a good idea. For a moment I even considered how upset my mother would be if she found out she raised a little thief. The thoughts of appearing "cool" and "brave" in front of Lisa quickly vanquished my apprehensions.

We walked into a pharmacy to stock up on free makeup. And within moments we were back outside with our handbags full of new stuff. An overwhelming rush of adrenaline made me feel invincible, and the thrill made it all the more appealing.

"What else do we need?" Lisa asked, not directing the question at me, but rather speaking to herself aloud. She paused. "I know, earrings."

I followed, adrenaline still racing through me. Now I was feeling eager and elevated.

We found ourselves at a stall that sold various pieces of jewelry. As we stupidly walked around pretending to be potential customers, I placed a pair of earrings in my handbag and prepared to walk out. About five steps in, the lady from the counter approached and asked to check my bag. I opened it up. She pulled out the earrings and immediately called security.

A million thoughts rushed through my head. I contemplated running, but before I could, I started to get faint. The fear of my mother finding out, paralyzed me. My face and body started to sweat. And apart from the stars I was seeing, my vision went pitch black.

Lisa tried to snap me out of it with a good shake. She kept saying, "Don't worry, I will take the blame."

By the time I found my balance again, we were headed for the center management office where the police awaited us.

Luckily, the shop owner did not press charges, but we were banned from the shopping center for two years. I knew this was a small consequence for our foolish actions.

The police drove us home and they immediately confronted my mother. They explained what had happened, and before leaving, one of the officers looked directly into my eyes.

"You need to figure out what you want in life," the male officer said very certainly. "Believe me, this path you're choosing, it doesn't end nicely."

His words resonated with me. I knew exactly what he meant and I believed him. As he turned to walk away, I unintentionally began to visualize his warning: jail, violence, death. I wanted to explain to him, I wasn't planning on doing bad things forever, and I wouldn't shoplift again. I yelled out to get his attention.

"I'm not planning on becoming a criminal!" I promised in a high pitch ascending tone. The officer stopped and turned around.

"That's the thing, most of them don't plan on it either. Don't make us come see you again."

I couldn't think of a way to respond to his statement in time, and the officers were gone before I knew it. Then I looked over at my mom. I could see the fury and disgust in her face while I cowardly awaited her response.

But she didn't say a word to me. Instead, she went into her room, lay on the bed and began to cry. I followed.

"Mom, I'm sorry, I won't do it again!" I begged, "Please stop crying."

"Julia, you will end up in jail. I don't know how to teach you better," she quietly murmured, implying it was all her fault. "Please leave me alone, I need some time."

Although I felt little remorse for most of my actions back then, on this occasion I felt horrible. I didn't want to leave her room, but it seemed like my presence was making it worse. So I walked across the hallway, into my room and sat on my bed to think:

"Why did you do it? Mom is such a hard working and honest woman. You are pathetic," I heard in my head. *"And now she thinks it's her fault, and the cops think you're a criminal. What are you doing?"*

Even in this situation, other peoples' opinions of me were more important than my destructive behavior.

I had an instant flashback to the day I stole the money from the magician busking in the street. I remember how I embarrassed my mom. She didn't raise me that way. And I wished I could take away her guilt. But it was too late, and I was the one that caused it.

A few days later, things continued to get worse.

"Sit down, Julia. I have seen you coming home smelling like alcohol and cigarettes for too long now," she began. I rolled my eyes and told her I didn't want to talk.

She picked up a pamphlet off the glass dining table.

"Julia, please, I know you are smoking marijuana. The symptoms are all right here," she said as she turned to the page titled "Symptoms of Users." Pretending not to care, I caught a glimpse of a few of the page's points:

- Agitation

- Tiredness

- Paranoia

I knew I had been caught, but there was no way I wanted to admit it. I stormed into my bedroom, packed a bag and decided to run away from home.

As I was frantically putting clothes into a gray backpack, my mother began to cry again.

"Please stop, Julia, I want to help you," she begged.

I didn't listen, and within a few minutes I was out the door. I heard my mother's deep sobbing as I walked down the hallway stairs, and I could feel the pain as if it were my own. And at that moment, I realized it was my own. I was tormenting us to avoid my own deep feelings of anguish from my father's death.

As I aimlessly walked with a heavy bag of clothes over my shoulder, I wondered why I put my mother through all of this. I didn't want to hurt her. But facing a difficult conversation with her was just too much to bear. I knew I was letting her down, but I was oblivious to the extent of the pain I was causing both of us. I justified it by thinking, *"Life let me down, so that's just how things worked."*

I found 40 cents in my wallet, which was enough to use the public payphone. I called my friend Alison, and she said it would be fine for me to stay with her. In fact, she was excited about it. And now I was, too.

For three days we ran around the streets high and drunk. We vandalized bus stops, lit a fire in a park and harassed strangers on the street for money and cigarettes.

On the third night, we stood at a busy roundabout in Kingsford. Drunk like idiots, we jumped around and cheered at any Holden Commodore that drove past and booed any Fords. Not that I was even passionate about either of those cars, but purely because Alison was. I was enjoying the sensation of causing chaos and projecting my inner anguish out onto the world.

We were quickly stopped by the police, thrown in the back of the wagon and taken to the police station.

After Alison and I were separated at the station, the officer called my mom, and she caught a taxi to pick me up. For a brief moment, I smiled and was happy to see her—almost as if I had forgotten that I had been arrested. And in truth, I had forgotten. This was happening so often that it now seemed normal to me.

As soon as we walked out onto the street, my mom started to yell at me. She was over it, frustrated and tired. Immediately I became defensive and walked the opposite way. She tried to follow me, so I started to run and quickly lost her.

With my mom out of sight, I sat on the ground and looked around me. It was the middle of the night and I was all alone. It was 1 a.m. again. I wished somebody would care or come to save me. Anyone to fill the empty void, tell me what to do... or even give me a hard time about how rude it was to make a late night phone call.

Lessons

TAKE RESPONSIBILITY IN YOUR RELATIONSHIPS

Fulfilment in all seven areas of life is the essence in Best Life-ing. There is no correct order to approach these areas. And the area of focus in which you wish to start may be different for you, depending on which area of life you feel least fulfilled.

The first area of life we will focus on is the Relational.

The Relational area of life covers your family and romantic relationships.

Family can be interpreted differently, this includes blood related, marriage or any other person you consider family. You may already feel that you are fulfilled in your family life for the most part; however, many people I've met, are also not—this is perfectly normal.

HOW DO YOU HANDLE DISAGREEMENTS AND FRUSTRATIONS?

We all have family issues from time to time, and there are ways to diffuse these situations when they arise. Family can be one of the most difficult areas to create fulfilment because generally you do not choose them and who they are.

When dealing with family, understand that harmony with your loved one is more important than the subject in most cases. If we separate the content of a disagreement from our ego and the need to be right, we find that harmony is almost always the end result that we seek. This, however, does not mean you remain silent when you disagree (more on this later in the Pineapple or no pineapple section).

Other people's beliefs, responses and conflicts are not in your control. But luckily it's not your job to control them. The only goal you have is to be fulfilled and feel good. When we really want peace of mind and harmony, we will get it.

You and the other person in the relationship create your circumstances together. Take responsibility and control of your emotions, and do what it takes to make it right, even if you do not agree on the subject (remember the Beliefs section).

Looking back on my relationship with my mother, I did not take responsibility for my feelings. Sure, I was a kid and acting out. But I also carried this poor behavior into some of my future relationships, which I will share soon. I wish I would have had the wisdom to understand that what I was feeling was not the world's fault.

Stop expecting others to agree with you or do things your way. Every person is unique and has their own thoughts, opinions and habits. Whether the other person does or does not understand you, makes no difference to you. Think about the actual act of understanding or not understanding. How another person perceives a disagreement or situation does not change your perception—unless you let it. It is much more effective to put energy into finding harmony than agreeing on a subject.

When you're in a disagreement, it is also important to identify why the subject is so preciously important to you. Anything that you dislike and strongly react to, is because you are seeing a quality in another that is one you have not yet accepted in yourself.

Your qualities, thoughts and behaviors that you have completely accepted, cannot bother you. Those that you have not yet accepted in yourself are the ones that get you fired up.

For example, you may hate liars, and when you see this quality in another person, it gets on your nerves. However, I am sure at some point in your life you have told a lie, probably multiple. This could be when you were younger to your teacher or parent, or a lie to your boss about being sick. It may have been to a friend when you cancelled your plans or didn't attend their baby shower, or to someone else about why you were running late.

We all have the same qualities, but we tend to place perimeters around the level in which they are acceptable to us, again based on our beliefs. Once we learn to accept that we all possess the same qualities in different levels, it becomes hard to get irritated with others possessing them, too.

Test yourself. Think of a family member who has often made you feel a specific type of negative emotion. Pinpoint what specific quality bothers you, and ask yourself:

When have I been (accurately or inaccurately) perceived to also possess this quality?

49

Get detailed with it and write down the specific time frames, day of the week and any details that you can remember, and be sure to go through all of the different periods in your life. When your list is big enough, you will accept that you also possess the same quality.

If you find yourself saying, "Yeah, but she lies about bigger things!" or whatever the quality is, keep working on your list; it means you are not quite there yet.

Romantic relationships can be a little bit different as there is more choice in who you select as your partner. However, the first step remains the same: take responsibility and control of your emotions.

You are always 100% of the problem or the solution.

Eckhart Tolle, an inspiring spiritual leader, has touched me through his books and teachings in many ways. In one of his seminars, he described that people tend to believe that a relationship is 50/50, but it is not. Because if a relationship were 50/50, then of course I always do the 50% that is right, and *you* would always do the 50% that is wrong and annoying. This is why all relationships require 100/100 effort to be harmonious.

THE 3 RELATIONSHIP ATTACHMENT STYLES

We need to understand that there are different attachment styles, which influence the way we behave and respond to others. There are a few different versions of the attachment theory and styles, but they mostly follow similar principles.

A great book that describes this perfectly and in great detail is called *Attached* by Amir Levine and Rachel S. F. Heller. I highly recommend reading it; to summarize:

There are three main styles of attachment in adults. None of these are right or wrong, they are simply the natural way in which we behave, based on our upbringings and the later relationships we experience.

1. The secure attachment style is the one we want to strive for. It is the best possible balance between caring enough, and not worrying too much. A secure person feels comfortable with intimacy, closeness and sharing their feelings without blame or negative emotion. A secure person can be proactive and predict their partner well, while being sensitive to his or her feelings They can read and respond to body language. A secure person doesn't stress about the relationship too much, and two secure partners rarely run into problems.

2. People with the anxious attachment style tend to spend a large amount of time analyzing how their partners fell, and if they love them. Anxious people tend to take their partners behaviour personally even if those words and actions have no association with the relationship itself. An anxious person constantly worries if they spend enough time together. Anxious people often question what is going on when their partners don't call back or make extra effort. If you are anxious, you may feel an unceasing need to spend time with your partner, or even need them to be readily available all the time. Anxious people tend to give up other priorities with the expectation that their partner will do the same.

3. People with the avoidant attachment style tend to value independence more than the relationship. Avoidant people struggle

to share their true feelings and respond well to the emotions and feelings of others. They tend to quickly blame others when things go wrong and don't assume much responsibility in the situation. They keep holding out for "the right one" and that makes it easy for them to find slight things that aren't good enough, and little ways that their partner is imperfect or irritating.

An anxious person should try to avoid dating an avoidant person (that'd be a crazy rollercoaster). Through strong communication just one partner in a relationship is being secure, helps the relationship blossom, and makes it more likely to work out.

Relationships that have partners with both anxious and avoidant attachment styles often experience many issues as one partner needs more affection and intimacy, while the other is not comfortable with these emotions and pulls away. However, if the relationship has at least one partner who has a secure attachment style, he or she can help their anxious or avoidant partner feel more secure, which can lead to a truly successful relationship. Your goal is to become the secure attachment style, and the key to this is effective communication.

By directly expressing your concerns and needs without blame or exaggeration (using words like "always" and "never"), you will feel better, while your partner will be relieved that he or she is not attacked or no longer has to guess what's wrong any more.

Effective communication is about finding a way to express your issues without blame or pointing fingers. Instead of saying, "You never text me" (blaming), be honest and say, "When I don't hear from you all day, it makes me feel insecure. How can we resolve this?"

Getting every one's expectations out on the table, gives you the opportunity to figure out together if they can all be met.

PINEAPPLE OR NO PINEAPPLE ON YOUR PIZZA?

A friend of mine was having relationship problems with her boyfriend. She would say things like:

"I want (this) but he doesn't want to commit, and I don't want to ask him about (this), because I can understand why he doesn't want (this), but at the same time I want the opposite (this)."

When the decision is complex and you have a higher emotional connection to it, seeing your options clearly can be difficult. It can be hard to see all the potential outcomes that may result from your choices. So, I put together a little metaphor for my friend, which can also be applied to pretty much any situation.

Imagine you go to the pizza shop because you are craving your favorite Hawaiian pizza with pineapple. You love pineapple on pizza. In fact, it's your favorite part, and this is the day in your diet routine that you get pizza! YES! You can't wait.

As you walk down to the shop, you begin to smell the flavors and imagine the taste of this pizza in your mouth. You're greeted by a very friendly man at the register who takes your order, but then gives you the shattering news. They are out of pineapple...forever.

You now have three choices to choose from.

1. Take the pizza without the pineapple. This analogy symbolizes a relationship where your partner doesn't display a desired quality or trait. For example, if he doesn't want to hold your hand, can you live without that "pineapple"? Or if she doesn't want to ever have children, can you live without that "pineapple"? Remember, there is no perfect pizza and you can still enjoy the sausage, mushrooms, pepperoni and other ingredients. You can still enjoy your partner's many other positive qualities—just not the pineapple. Can you live without it? The answers vary for each individual. Decide on yours.

2. Choose a different pizza, meaning compromise. Come to an agreement in the middle that works for you both.

3. Or your other option is, go and get a taco! Accept that what you want, doesn't make the other person happy. Go and find the qualities you are looking for in someone else who also wants the same things.

If you are searching for love, or any meaningful relationship at all, think of this analogy when you don't feel fulfilled with the other person's values or behaviors. Only you have the power to make *you* happy.

Diary Entry

November 13th, 2018 – Atlanta, Georgia

THE PERFECT FAMILY

Our minds can create and believe in realities that do not even exist the way we think they will.

For many of my younger years, I wished, dreamed of and wondered what it would be like to have a bigger and more perfect family. You know, like the ones you see on TV. I was convinced I was missing out on something. But later, life showed me this interesting perspective.

After moving to the USA, I lived with what seemed to be the perfect dream family that I had always wished for. They had the beautiful big house, two healthy and hard working parents, four children and two beagles.

The kids were talented. One was completing her college degree, another was a 17-year-old soccer player who was just accepted into the professional Atlanta United soccer team. The third brother worked for the parents' company, and the last was a cute little nine-year-old who was very smart for his age.

It didn't take long to see that even this perfect family wasn't exactly what I imagined. But they didn't know they were perfect, and the real version came with more dimensions. They, too, had disagreements at the dinner table, fights over irrelevant things, overreactions, tantrums, tears and struggles.

They, too, had moments of exhaustion, fear, anger and not belonging. Could it be true that this perfect family had problems that were not so different from my imperfect family?

Their perfect existence was not real, nor had it ever been. I had spent all these years wishing that I had something that didn't even exist. It was a fabricated story designed to do nothing more than to make me feel bad. Like something was missing, when it never actually was.

My point is, we have all experienced moments where we are wishing for something that doesn't exist. There is no good without bad, no success without failure. The feeling in between those is "numb."

Have you ever wanted a different relationship only to get it and realize it's not as perfect as it seemed?

This perfectly not-so-perfect family showed me that I was never really missing anything. Sure, their names were different than my own family, there were more of them at the dining table and their house was bigger. But every argument, emotion and opinion seemed similar to those that happened in my own household.

Tonight, the 17-year-old started an argument during dinner; it was about studying for a test. Once he stormed out after cursing us all out, the parents were extremely embarrassed and apologized profusely. I laughed as I remembered being that 17-year-old.

"Don't worry, my family dinner table wasn't much different. On that note, please excuse me; I need to call and apologize to my mom."

KEY POINTS:

1. Always being right in a disagreement is unattainable. Remember that harmony is always more important than the subject, even if that harmony means that you both thoughtfully agree to disagree.

2. Take responsibility and control of how you feel. You are either 100% of the problem or the solution in your relationships.

3. The negative emotions that you feel towards other people are qualities that you have not yet accepted in yourself.

4. The secure attachment style is the most advantageous. Work on becoming secure by expressing your insecurities (ah, the irony) through effective communication.

5. The opposing situation is not really the way you may imagine it, nor is it usually what you think it will be.

ACTION STEPS:

1. Think about the last time you were in a disagreement with a family member, spouse or significant other. Was the subject more important than achieving harmony with your loved one, or do you just need to figure out whether you can live without the "pineapple"?

2. Try to have a new conversation with this person about your issue, now knowing if you can or can't live without the behavior or quality changing. In this new conversation, be sure to remain in the secure attachment style.

3. Evaluate your conversation. Did you come to an agreement that works for you both? Are you happy to enjoy your life without the "pineapple"? Or are you going to go and get a taco instead?

Chapter Three

SHOULDER SHRUGS TO CEO

AREA OF LIFE 2/7: INTELLECTUAL

All of the other kids' parents couldn't stand me, pulling out all the stops to forbid their children from associating with me; but this made me even "cooler" in their kids' eyes. Somehow, I would coordinate groups of kids to run away and roam the streets with Alison and I; my mother would often get abusive phone calls from the raging parents.

"Keep your awful Julia away from my daughter!" They would say. Simon's mom was the only exception; Lea was always warm, kind and welcoming when I came over. She never judged and always graced us with love.

Running away from home constantly (and being the ring leader) obviously had its challenges—you know, my mom wasn't exactly funding it.

I wanted a job. Not because I wanted to save money for and buy anything in particular, but because I despised waiting and relying on someone else to provide me with the things I wanted. So I lied about my age and got a job at my local McDonald's.

By now I was really struggling at school. I rarely attended classes and my grades had become tragic, to put it nicely. I was asked to meet with the principal, and I showed up to the appointment high. I didn't really care about what he had to say or the consequences. At this stage, I had very little, if not zero, respect for the law.

The principal sat me down in his office, beside my mother.

"Julia, what is it that you want out of life?" he began.

I shrugged my shoulders.

"Well, the way you are going, you are not going to make it very easy for yourself," the principal continued. "Your attendance is well below what is acceptable, and your grades have dropped dramatically. I am concerned. When you joined this school, you were a very promising student."

His words meant nothing to me. I sat in silence waiting for him to get to the point so that this conversation could end.

"I have a second chance for you," he said as he stared at me so forcefully I couldn't turn away. "I would like you to consider repeating year nine."

"What?!" I finally reacted.

"I think it would be for the best," the principal responded.

My first thoughts were, "*I can't repeat, everyone will think I am stupid. How will I face the other kids who are now going to be a year above me? I'm not going to study in the class with all the younger kids.*"

"No, I'm not doing it!" I yelled.

"Unfortunately, this is your only option if you want to stay in this school. I really suggest you do it and that you try to take school more seriously this time," he said.

My next thought was, *"I'm never coming back!"*

Right then and there, I dropped out of school at the end of year nine without completing my school certificate.

This was one of my mother's worst nightmares; she was absolutely devastated. She was so determined to give us a good education in hopes of offering us a head start in life. She begged me to stay or even go to a different school, but despite all of her efforts, I refused.

HOW MCDONALD'S BEGAN TO CHANGE MY LIFE

Dropping out of school was a reality check for me. I quickly came to the realization that I needed to do something with my time.

To my surprise, I actually enjoyed my new job at McDonald's; I had made new friends and was picking up the job tasks quickly. My boss constantly gave me appreciative and constructive feedback, and this inspired me and challenged me to do better.

Within a few months, they offered to put me through a traineeship for a Certificate III in Retail Operations. This learning environment was different; people were encouraging and supportive, and although the job was labor intensive at times, I felt happy.

I found that I was good with both the theory and practical aspects of the traineeship, and I became increasingly intrigued with the systems and operations of the business. I absorbed myself in getting all of the book work done, and I wanted to learn everything there was to know about the organization.

After my shifts, I would stay late in the lobby, working on the bookwork. In my spare time, I would ask questions and hang around the workplace, learning tasks and processes that I didn't know. Managers literally had to kick me out of the store to make me go home (after 24 hours I think they wanted me to shower). I was obsessed; it took me only three months to complete the program that should have taken twelve. My boss was impressed with my dedication and ability.

This was probably my first real taste of inspiration. All I wanted to focus on was excelling at work, learning everything and getting promoted. I didn't actually have a plan that went much further than that; all I knew was that I finally enjoyed something. I hadn't felt that in a long time. What's more, this new effortless learning was easy; my enjoyment fueled my effort, and this powered me to excel.

Soon I was promoted to management. I was so proud of myself, this small accomplishment made me feel like my life finally had some meaning. Not because of the promotion itself, but because I was now part of a team and contributing—feeling wanted and needed. And it all started through the magic of just one person believing in me, believing that I was good at something.

So there I was, the youngest manager on the team, and in the region. Not only had I achieved some success, but I loved my job. Unfortunately, other people didn't see it the same way.

DEALING WITH MCDONALD'S SHAMING

When I'd speak to Simon and a few other classmates from school, they would tell me stories about the other kids making fun of me for dropping out.

"She's a dropout," they would laugh. "She dropped out to be a McDonald's manager!"

My happy reality was yet again challenged by what other people thought. And again, it felt like what I was doing was wrong or "not good enough"— *but why? I was happy, did people just not want me to be happy?*

I soon began to feel ashamed of working at McDonald's because that was the general consensus of people who didn't work there: McDonald's employees are losers. I allowed people who had no idea what it felt like to be doing, living and feeling what I felt, to tell me how to feel about my life.

"She's going to work at McDonald's her whole life," they would say in a degrading tone, as if that were a bad thing, implying that I had no chance of achieving success. P.S. I know many people who have chosen to pursue a career at McDonald's that are extremely successful, wealthy and abundant people who live fulfilled lives.

Regardless of how upsetting it was for me to hear their judgments, negative perceptions and verdicts for my life, I had no real choice but to let it go. Thankfully, with the help of my good friend Simon, I got through it.

One morning, Simon called me fuming on the phone from the scene he witnessed during roll call. My name was called and a few of the kids started laughing. Then one girl yelled out:

"She dropped out to be a McDonald's Manager!"

"Bro, shut up! She's killing it at McDonald's," Simon interrupted. "Let her do what she wants. Why do you all need to be such dicks behind her back."

Simon received a warning for swearing, but he didn't care. He was furious about the situation. This was another moment where Simon was a great friend, not because of what he said to the class, but because he believed in me and recognized my happiness. I encourage you to be like Simon. Being a great friend to people can be life-changing for them.

The opinions of school classmates, adults and ex-teachers were becoming easier to ignore, but then the worst of this challenge emerged—the McDonald's customers.

McDonald's had some of the worst customers. I say this after working in bars, diners and high end restaurants later in life. At McDonald's, I saw my fair share of customers who seemed to have a sense of entitlement. As if by eating there, they were granted permission to treat the workers in a degrading manner, unashamedly.

Soon, I learned not to care what people thought of me working at McDonald's. In fact I was so interested in understanding people that I started analyzing why they acted and felt the way they did about McDonald's employees. I took mental notes as I observed customers' traits and how people reacted to me differently depending on whether I wore my employee uniform or my street clothes. It was like a game to me.

What I saw was astounding. On one occasion, a customer in his early twenties was straight-out abusing a colleague of mine. I mean abusing, like she had lost his first-born child (when in reality, all she did was forget to put his BBQ sauce in the bag).

This man was really digging into my coworker, using all sorts of profanities and calling her and everybody else who worked at McDonald's stupid. Ironically, the girl he was yelling at was completing her Bachelor's in Psychology and was far from stupid. I approached to calm him down and try to help.

"Another dumb bitch!" he yelled out. I paused, composed myself and then helped him resolve the problem (i.e., I gave him the missed BBQ sauce, and he left).

Two nights later, I was at the local bar (yes, I had a fake ID) and I instantly recognized the same guy standing across from me, except this time I wasn't wearing my McDonald's uniform. I was dressed up with a full head of makeup. We made eye contact.

"Do I know you from somewhere?" he asked.

"I don't think so, never seen you before," I lied.

"Oh sorry," he said as he began to turn away, just moving his head slightly to face his buddy on the left. He stopped, turned back to me, "Hey, you're very beautiful. We should hang out sometime, can I get your number?"

I nearly threw up on myself, metaphorically speaking. Guess the makeup and outfit made me *not* a "dumb bitch" anymore.

I was learning, just in my own way, to use my practical experiences to collect information. But I needed another component which I didn't know yet. This was to fall in love with learning.

And like clockwork, as the saying goes, "When the student is ready, the teacher appears"— along came my future boss, friend and mentor Bernard Kelly.

THE FIRST TIME I MET BERNARD

I officially met Bernard at a work Christmas party. I had heard of him prior to this night, as he was a senior leader in our company. We had been briefly introduced, and we sat down outside. He spoke to other people at the table and then addressed me.

"Was it Jodie…Jessica…?" Bernard began.

"Julia," I corrected him, accepting the fact that Bernard had no reason to remember my name.

"Julia, sorry, that's a very lovely dress you are wearing," he said.

"Thank you."

"How much did it cost you?"

"Um, I don't know, like $700," I replied, a little thrown by his question.

"That's a lot of money for a dress," Bernard said, "so what is your big dream in life?"

"I'm going to be the CEO of McDonald's," I replied surely. It's crazy how in just a short year since the conversation when my principal had asked me a similar question, the answer had changed so much.

"Oh really?" he laughed, "and do you have a plan of how you are going to be the CEO?"

"Yeah! I'm going to work hard, learn everything and get promoted," I replied.

"That's a good start," he said. "But you know, to become the CEO it is going to take a lot more than just hard work and learning."

"Like what?" I asked.

"Well, for a start, there are going to be sacrifices, and you are going to have to develop the ability to delay instant gratification."

"OK," I had no idea what he was talking about, but I agreed anyway.

"It's a big dream, I like it," he began to elaborate. "But to be the CEO, you will need to absorb more knowledge than just what you learn in the restaurants. You will need to read a lot of books."

"I don't really like reading books that much," I replied. "You know, I just don't focus when I'm reading. The words go in my head but I can't really make much sense of them."

"With practice you will, it's a very great advantage," Bernard assured. "You can learn a lot about someone's life and experiences in just the seven hours it takes to read their book."

"That's true," I replied, pondering if this was possible for me.

"If you want to be an interesting person, read books!" he reinforced. "And the books you read will change your life."

"My life doesn't need changing," I laughed.

"You're young, just wait until the temptations and outside pressures of life kick in. You will be faced with many choices. And if you really want to be the CEO, you will need to make all decisions toward that. This is going to involve a lot of sacrifice," Bernard concluded.

"Pfft, what does he know about what I've been through? Sacrifices! That's been my whole life," I thought.

I didn't know it then but Bernard was right: life did get in the way later; I chose instant gratification and I didn't make the sacrifices necessary to become the CEO. Though if I had, how would my life be different today? Would I have learned what it takes to create fulfilment?

Many, many years later, Bernard and I sat on the couch in my rock bottom moment. Almost a decade had passed and his advice didn't change: read books to build your knowledge.

You gain a huge advantage when you develop an appreciation for learning. As humans, we have an enormous need for growth and expansion, and one way to accomplish this is by building on your intellect.

Without continuous growth and self-improvement, Best Life-ing cannot be achieved. Yes, there may be moments of inconsistency, but as your passion for learning grows over the years, you'll be able to build your knowledge and incorporate it into your daily life.

Lessons

WHY YOU SHOULD READ BOOKS EVERY SINGLE DAY

"If you are willing to choose self improvement and change mentality, the sky's the limit!" —John C Maxwell, *The Five Levels of Leadership.*

The Intellectual area of life is one that can be easily forgotten when we get caught up in our day to day tasks. Learning new things feels confusing, uncomfortable and challenging, so it is easy to get stuck in our comfort zones.

The brain is a muscle that needs to be exercised regularly, just like every other muscle in your body. And in order to have fulfilment in this area, you must continue to intellectually challenge yourself and grow.

Thankfully, it's in our nature to grow and evolve as humans. And when we try to resist expansion, we naturally feel incomplete. My principal was right. I took the harder road to learning. And kids if you're reading this, I don't recommend dropping out! But if you have, or if you experience learning challenges, it is not the end of the road.

Even today in a classroom environment, I struggle; and exams freak me out. Find a way that works for you. This could be reading books, learning online or actively engaging in a challenging activity.

Fall in love with learning by learning about what you love. Reading books about your favorite topics or even novels can help. Pick up your smartphone and search articles, videos, stories and blogs on the topic. You don't necessarily need a goal or an outcome. Just start to learn about something you like.

Several years ago, I replaced listening to music in the car with audiobooks, switched out watching TV for reading books and changed my social media scrolling to brain training games or research time. I still watch shows, listen to music and use social media, but in scheduled time—and much less regularly, rather than aimlessly wasting hours on it.

These simple changes gave me an abundance of clarity because my brain was no longer polluted with an overload of useless information and opinions. It also freed up my time, allowing me to discover a new appreciation for relaxation and enjoyment for learning.

If you're unsure where to start, follow your interests; this will help you discover what you value. One indication that something is high on your values is if you love learning about it.

Another incredible aspect of learning is that it constantly challenges your opinions and belief systems. Books provide stories and lessons of people's lifelong accomplishments. And there is great benefit in the organized information that has been compiled for you from the author's life.

Why is reading books so important? There is a wealth of knowledge in every one's story and people sharing their experiences in their own creative way.

You could learn 50 years of experience on a subject, or feel inspired to take action from someone else's story and accomplishments in as little as 5 hours!

A book is not easy to write (believe me, I know). Like other dreams it takes time, research, discipline and imagination. It takes courage to share personal stories and a lot of work to organize everything you know into an understandable guide. People who write books have something to offer you. These people are also usually successful in their own pursuits.

Whatever you are struggling with, don't know how to do or haven't yet experienced, the answer lies in a book written by someone who has. And I challenge you to start reading at least one book per month. From this moment on, read any book you start, to the end—even if you don't like it. That's discipline.

The average book is eight hours long. So, by investing only 30 minutes per day, you can get through one almost every fortnight, or 26 per year. Imagine the depth of knowledge in 26 books.

There is never a shortage of books or an end to the possibilities. Successful people read books. If you want to be successful in any area of life or on any topic, pick up a book and finish it!

In 2015 I set a goal to read one book a month. You know how many I finished? Zero. Why? Because I didn't see the value in reading and I didn't prioritize it. Yes, I made the same reasons up in my mind: no time, too busy, can't concentrate, (insert excuse here). But they were just that. Excuses. My life didn't get any easier the following year. The reality is, back then I just didn't care enough about expanding my knowledge and learning what I didn't know. The only book I had time for was "Facebook" and, to be honest, these days it's hard to find much on there except mind-numbing junk.

The following year, I finished 37 books without having an extra hour in my day. There's no magic formula to it. I simply just read on the train instead of scrolling through my phone, and listened to audiobooks instead of learning the lyrics to the latest hit songs.

Diary Entry

July 27th, 2018 – Tamarindo, Costa Rica

BEACH BOOK CLUB

Costa Rica is the most breathtaking place I have traveled to, a place where the rivers cascading down waterfalls blend seamlessly into rainforests which mingle with the beaches. Here, the sun ignites crystal blue skies as the great mountains loom around the sides.

Gaby was a local that I met on the first night. We sat by the fire watching the gentle ocean waves roll in as we admired the silk-soft white sand.

Gaby and I had many deep conversations about life. We discussed the differences of our countries, upbringing and personal beliefs. She and I had a lot in common, and our conversations lasted hours late into the night.

"You know so much about self love and alignment. Do they teach this topic in your schools?" Gaby asked.

"No," I laughed, "but they should!"

"Then how do you know about it? And how do you know what is true?"

"Just by reading many books on the subject, then you see the common similarities and you can form your own belief," I replied. "Most books have a similar message. They just use different words, stories and labels to describe their message."

"I have noticed that," she said, pondering the thought.

"What about you?" I asked. "You're very aligned also, and you are doing very well for yourself. From our conversations you seem to be fulfilled in everything you are doing."

"Simple. I read a lot of books, too," she smiled.

KEY POINTS:

1. To grow, we need to continue to challenge ourselves intellectually. Expansion is necessary.

2. Seek ways to love learning. Start by learning about something you love or enjoy. Learn your own way. Break it down into manageable chunks, for example 30 minutes per day, and this will make any task feel a lot easier.

3. If you are not exercising your brain, you will feel intellectually incomplete.

4. Challenge what you think you know by researching the opposite.

5. Successful people read books.

ACTION STEPS:

1. Make it a goal to read or listen to the audio of one book per month. If a book is 300 pages long, that's usually about 4.5 hours of audio, which is 10 pages a day, or 9 minutes a day of audio book time. I'm sure you can do that on your way to work!

2. This action step is a fun one. It incorporates what you learned about belief in the previous chapter and the Intellectual area of life. Choose a viewpoint opposite to one you hold and debate the issue with a friend or family member. Sounds difficult, right? That's the point! Focusing attention on ideas that are different to your beliefs can improve intellectual wellness. Naturally, we tend to only focus our attention on opinions, beliefs and facts that are aligned with our perspective. When you expose the mind to opposing information, it provides the opportunity for the mind to expand, grow and grasp new information.

Chapter Four

DEATH AT MY DOORSTEP

AREA OF LIFE 3/7: SPIRITUAL

Spirituality is your version of faith, religion, connection or oneness. I encourage you to have some form of spirituality in your pursuit of Best Life-ing. Fast-forward to when I turned 23, when an innate desire to connect with a higher power awakened in me.

Dan and I had been living together for over a year; we had been seeing each other for two years prior to moving in together. And he was the closest person in my life at that time.

On August 10th, 2012, I woke to another cold winter morning in Sydney. As usual, I made my coffee, sat on the couch and began to scroll through Facebook. Dan sat on the couch beside me, doing the same.

Suddenly, I was jarred out of my routine when I noticed a post from Simon that stopped my entire world—like a movie on a laptop, interrupted by the press of the spacebar. I was in disbelief. The post was my discovery that his mother had just passed away. Instantly I felt a source of distress come over me; I knew the feeling very well. *How could this be possible? Simon had never mentioned that his mother was sick.*

"Simon," I rang immediately, "what's going on?"

"Come over, man," he replied. His voice had never sounded like this, and I immediately knew the answer to my next question.

"Wait, it's true?" I panicked as my eyes began to fill with tears. "What happened to Lea?"

"Just come down," Simon replied. I could feel the utter despair of his shattered energy through the phone.

"OK, I'm on my way."

Without hesitation, I jumped off the couch and grabbed my things.

"What happened?" Dan spotted the tears and panic on my face, and he quickly stood up and walked over.

"I gotta go, Simon's mom is gone! Out of nowhere!" I cried.

"Oh shit," he said as he caught up to me in the hallway near the door. He put both of his palms around my shoulders and looked consolingly into my watery eyes. "You ok?"

"No, but I'm sure Simon is worse, so I need to be...." I replied, still scrambled by the reality of what was going on.

"Just be strong, Juju," Dan said firmly. "He is gonna need you right now...just...be...strong."

I nodded silently, my lips quivering as I held back the tears. I knew I had to hold it together; there was no other option. I had to be strong for my friend.

As I drove the road to his house, 40 minutes seemed to pass by quickly. My mind was racing with countless questions and thoughts: *How could this have happened? How am I going to help? How is Simon dealing with this? What do I say? I need to keep it together. You can't cry, you need to be strong. I don't give a shit how you feel, Julia, Simon just lost his mother!*

An overwhelming sense of gloom and uncertainty consumed me; I badly wanted this to be a sick joke. I literally checked my phone, hoping to see it was April fool's day. It wasn't. And as I got closer to Simon's home, I felt as if I was out of my body, as if I was observing myself drive, watching my life happen to me from somewhere else. The house appeared to come toward me, like it was on a conveyor belt; I felt completely out of control.

Stepping out of the car, I noticed that I had no memory of driving here. Everything was vague, like a slumber. I forced myself back into reality and advanced unknowingly into the house. Simon sat there on the couch in his room, breathing, but everything else about him was missing.

"Hey bro, thanks so much for coming!" he said as he got up to give me a hug.

"Of course," I replied, trying to hold back the feeling of the inevitable breakdown welling up inside me.

"Man, I just can't believe she's really gone," he sighed as he sipped on a Corona, his eyes fixated on the ground.

"I know, me too," I said softly, placing my arm around his shoulder. "How did this happen, Simon?"

"I really don't know, it was all so sudden," he began. "One moment she was fine. The next I got a call from my brother, and she was gone."

The words left his mouth along with the courage to hold it together. His grief engulfed the room like a livid plague. But I had to be strong. I had to fight my own sadness a little bit longer.

"I'm so sorry, Simon," was all I could say. I wished I could have had something better, some good news, a miracle or even just a more reassuring sentence, like he always had for me when I needed it. But I didn't believe there was one. There was no happy ending, and I *couldn't* promise truthfully that it was going to be okay. I tightened all of the muscles in my face to regain control and muster artificial strength.

I sat with him all afternoon while the news spread, which attracted a large gathering. The house soon filled with love, support and hope. But I could feel my emotional collapse coming. I couldn't do it. I had to leave.

"I'm gonna go," I said softly, thinking he'd hold up better if he didn't see me break down. "Walk me out?"

"Yeah man, thanks so much for coming. It means a lot," Simon replied as we headed towards the door.

"All good!" I yelled back as I jumped in my car. But as soon as I started the engine, the feelings of utter grief, hopelessness and despair collided into me like a freight train. By the end of the street, I pulled over to break down and cry.

When I turned the key to my apartment, the sound of Dan's rapid footsteps greeted me.

"How did it go?" Dan asked softly, realizing he didn't need an answer as I plummeted to the ground.

Every emotion exploded out of me from the depths of my soul, liberated like a raging fire, devouring oxygen from a puncture in its formerly vacuum sealed chamber. I sobbed so hard; the viscous exhales wouldn't let me catch my breath.

"I can't do this anymore," I wailed. " I don't want to be here."

Dan held me in both arms so tight, "It's okay."

"No it's not!" I continued. "I don't want to be here and watch any more people die around me. I can't do it, I'm not strong enough. I don't want to live. It's not fair, why leave a boy with no parents? Why!"

"Shhhhh," he tried to calm me. "Jules, just breath, I know it's hard."

I couldn't stop. The thoughts were so ruthless, and the tears emptied me dry. Dan held me in his arms the entire time, and I could feel his strength as I fell apart.

"I will never argue with my mom again if you just bring Lea back!" I wailed aloud. Dan knew I wasn't addressing him in my statement.

Dan tried to extinguish the blaze with his words, but he couldn't calm me down.

"Come on," he said powerfully. "I wanna take you somewhere, let's go for a drive."

"Where?" I sobbed. I was empty; I had no energy to move.

"A spot of mine, come." He pulled me up off the ground with both hands. I felt dizzy.

Without a word, he drove to the untold location.

In the passenger seat of the car, I sat hopeless, staring out the window as I watched the world carry on as normal. Car horns beeping, couples walking along the sidewalk and the sound of music wafted through the city streets. To the world outside, everything was the same. But for me, my world was upside down.

Dan drove us through the city, and slowly the busyness of the world began to fade away. Less cars, less people and more silence, until...

"Look up," he said as we arrived.

"Wow!" I gasped.

The footpath along a long, dark tree-lined road was lit up by an otherworldly glow of enchanting fairy lights. They resembled bright stars, as if each twinkling light was plucked from the sky. A second glimpse revealed the trees edged into a lustrous water, where the motionless boats were resting for the night.

The moon was traced perfectly onto the sky canvas, awakening the night with its vivid elegance. Bright city buildings flickered their lights as their reflection glistened on the river. The sound of a waterfall chanted a calming spell to assure the chaotic sounds of the outside world could not follow, casting the most serene silence around us—as though this place and this moment was reserved exclusively for the two of us.

The world was peaceful, still and asleep. I smiled, but only a little.

"I knew a couple of fairy lights could cheer you up," Dan joked in relief as we stepped out of the car.

A wooden rail surrounding the perfectly trimmed grass invited us to sit down.

"Close your eyes," he said, taking hold of my hand. "Let's talk to God."

"I've never prayed before," I whispered.

"Shh, close your eyes," he calmed me. I did as he said.

Dan said a prayer, first thanking God for our blessings, then asking for love, forgiveness and guidance for Simon and I.

He finished his words with an Amen. I slowly opened my eyes and somehow I felt light.

To this day I can't explain it. I don't even want to describe it as a feeling because it goes way beyond that. I just knew that something greater than us was making its presence known in that moment.

For a split second, Dan's energy was one with mine, and we were both connected to something magnificent. It wasn't a feeling, it was a certainty.

Certainty that we were exactly in the right place.

Certainty this was the right time.

Certainty we were safe.

Certainty that there were no accidents and that everything was going to be okay.

My doubt had subsided. I felt whole; the air was love and the moment was simplicity. I knew that life outside of this moment still wasn't perfect, but it seemed irrelevant because I was here in *this* moment. The only one that mattered for now.

This feeling was presence. I can't confirm if it was God, The Universe, another higher power or even just my imagination that brought me that feeling, but the connection brought me peace.

"Thank you, Dan," I said peacefully as I collected myself and wiped more tears from my face.

"Anytime, kiddo," he replied. "You know I'll always look out for you."

The coming weeks settled the intensity of my emotions. "Time heals all," Dan would quote.

"How much time?" I would think in response. 12 years hadn't yet healed the pain for me.

REVISITING MY DAD'S GRAVE

One morning, I woke up and nothing could stop me from going to the cemetery. This was strange because seeing my dad's grave stirred up painful emotions. I hated it. I would feel overwhelmed with the grief, sadness and regret that I dreaded, but I decided to act on this impulse anyway.

I had no idea why I was going, but I felt a need to find out. Though I had no spiritual or religious beliefs at this time, something compelled me to go.

But then, when I pulled up to the cemetery gates, I was hit with an immediate problem. I couldn't remember where to go. I had always struggled with direction, but I also didn't visit dad's grave often; and it wasn't like I could just type the address into the GPS.

There were only four turns I needed to make once I drove through the gate, but I made all the wrong ones. I drove around for an hour until I was so lost that I couldn't even guess what turn to take next. Nothing looked familiar, and it wasn't; everything had changed since I had last been there.

I stopped the car, frustrated—another day another tear. "Why?" I yelled out. "Why don't I know where he is?"

I felt ashamed, angry at myself. I remembered how Dan turned to God two weeks prior. I thought I would try to do the same.

"Dear God," I closed my eyes and put my palms together. "Forgive me for everything wrong that I've done. Thank you for blessing me with all that you have. Please, help me find my dad."

Guilt brought tears to my eyes for a moment. Suddenly, a slight distraction of a bird landing on the car hood stopped the feeling. I was there again: the present, where nothing else mattered and nothing was really wrong outside of my thoughts. I was just sitting in my car... sitting... *being*. This time it wasn't certainty that I knew, it was guidance.

Turn the car back on. Drive straight to the end, turn left at the cafe, turn right at 24B, keep going....I felt so I followed. It wasn't a voice, but something was speaking. As if just the right frequencies were being sent to me.

"Third row, I know where I am!" I replied aloud, knowing I was talking to myself.

I didn't hear a voice out loud or even an otherworldly voice in my head. It was my voice in my head—but how did my voice suddenly know the directions?

I sat down on the cold gravel footpath by my father's grave: a pile of dirt, with a wooden stick, labeled using a gray metal plate with his name and a number. It sickened me to look at. I despised the fact that it had been more than a decade, and we still couldn't afford to put a proper monument in his honor.

I calmed down and let the hours pass by as I simply sat and stared. No thoughts, no questions, just stillness. I enjoyed it so much that I didn't notice the sun setting beside me.

"Miss!" I heard a real voice shout from across the lawn. "The gates shut at sunset, you have about five more minutes."

I stood up in a hurry and slowly glided to the car. Back to reality, a place I liked less. Thoughts and questions about my dad quickly made their way back into my mind; they took over my stillness. I was jarred by these thoughts immediately, but I couldn't stop them from racing back in. I needed to get the answers.

There were many times I contemplated asking my mother these questions but thought that I shouldn't: *What kind of man was he? What was his favorite song? What was his favorite drink at the bar? And what kind of father would he have been?*

I didn't ask, because I assumed it would hurt her. I used to think about how hard it would be to lose your husband and survive all of the things that she went through.

When he died, I saw depression consume her, lying in bed for weeks at the start, followed by the multiple tears I had caused her to shed. I didn't want to bring those memories back again. The thing is, my mother's depression had passed many years ago. She had healed and came to acceptance; it was only me who hadn't. My assumptions and fears were the only thing preventing me from doing the same.

Aside from this, I never asked these questions aloud, because I was afraid of the answers. What if he wasn't a good man?

I stopped at a bar and ordered a bottle of wine with one glass. *Call her* or *don't call her* was my only decision. The fears and "what-ifs" circled and circled, but each glass of wine slowed them down.

I was as ready as I'd ever been. The phone was in my hand already, and one swipe up was the key to unlock a treasure chest of answers to the questions that had been driving me nuts. Answers that I wasn't sure I was ready to hear.

"Mom, I want to know about dad," I said in a shaky voice.

"Oh darling, of course, what would you like to know?" she replied warmly.

"What was his favorite food, what drink did he order at the bar?" It was clear I was hurting.

Caught off guard, my mom slowly began to answer the questions.

I started to cry, as quietly as possible, wiping the salty waterfalls off my face.

"Don't cry, my darling," my mother continued, knowing I was trying to hide my sadness. "What else would you like to know?"

"What kind of a man was he?" I sobbed.

"He was an amazing man!" she replied without hesitation. "He was gentle and patient, kind and warm hearted. He was forever seeking ways to help others, even when they didn't ask for it."

How could each word be beautiful to hear, yet so painful to feel at the same time?

"He was always running a million miles an hour like you," she went on, "working long days and being an amazing provider for his family. He loved you kids so much."

"Mom, I just want to meet him," I broke down. "I just want to have *one* beer with him, that's all I want in this life."

"Oh Julia, I know," she said. Even over the phone, I could hear the hurt in her voice. "Come over, I will give you a hug."

"I will mom, just not tonight, I've got to go," I hung up and tried to pull myself together. I didn't know the next step, and the only thing I wanted was impossible.

I knew I needed help.

BUILDING A SPIRITUAL CONNECTION

I met with Terri at the youth service center. I happened to be there as a favor for an employee, but I did not anticipate what this experience was about to do for me.

I arrived at Terri's psychology office. All I had to do was answer a few questions and make sure Terri knew that this employee was working, safe and up-to-date with her studies, so that this employee didn't have to stay with the department of children services.

Terri gave off an incredible energy; I could feel it right away. She greeted me and showed me where to sit down. We did our introductions, followed by a series of small talk questions.

"Where do you work?" she began.

"McDonald's," I smiled.

"Do you have any siblings?" Terri asked.

"Yes, a younger sister," I responded.

"And what is your relationship like?"

"It's OK, we try to see each other when we can," I replied hesitantly. What did this have to do with the employee I was here representing? I wondered.

"OK, how about your parents?"

"My mother and I fight a lot, but it has been better than when I was younger," I replied, attempting to avoid the next inevitable question.

"What do you fight about?"

"I'm not sure, she's always on my case about something. She starts the fights. I just have a short temper," I said, instantly wondering if I was giving too much away.

"And your father? Is he in the picture?" she asked softly.

"No, he died when I was younger," I answered. The usual heavy rock started to form in the back of my throat. It was the same uncomfortable feeling I had whenever I discussed my dad with anyone.

"I'm sorry," she said in a perfectly empathic, yet unchanged nature. "How did it happen?"

"He got sick," I began. As usual, this conversation caused my voice to shake and eyes to fill with tears. "He had a stroke, got dementia and passed away."

"And how do you feel about it?" Terri asked, still neutral but gracefully passing me a tissue.

"I'm fine, it was a long time ago. Just don't really like talking about it," I said, wiping my eyes.

"How long ago did this happen?"

"12 years ago," I replied.

She finished writing her notes and, with the touch of one finger, adjusted the round glasses sitting on her nose. She hadn't asked any questions about Olivia, the employee I was there to discuss.

"Would you like to hear what I'd like to share with you?" she asked impartially.

"Sure," I replied.

"I could be wrong, but I think you haven't quite come to accept what happened to your father," Terri began. "I see right now you find it very hard to talk about. But with a few of my techniques, we could get through that, together. Would you like to try that with me?"

"Um, OK," I said, puzzled because I wasn't expecting it. Then a thought: *"Wait, why are you saying "yes"? How are you going to pay for that?"*

"And McDonald's," Terri continued. "I don't see you doing that forever."

"What do you mean? I love it there, I'm going to be the CEO," I said, more enthusiastically.

"I'm not saying it's bad, I just sense your energy. I think you have something else to give the world," she said.

"No," I dismissed. "I'm really happy there."

"OK, so I'll see you in two weeks?" Terri confirmed.

"What about Olivia? Isn't that why I am here?" I asked.

"Olivia? Oh," Terri replied. "For Olivia's case, you just need to fill out the form at the front desk and sign off as the employer."

"Wait, so I wasn't supposed to come and speak to you?" I clarified.

"No, I thought you wanted to," she laughed.

"Oh no... I mean, yes, I liked talking to you," I scrambled. "But doesn't that mean that I need to pay you for this session?"

"No," she laughed again. "We have a free service for people under 24."

I was 23. What were the chances of everything aligning so harmoniously? Turns out that I was in the wrong place at the right time.

I walked back to my car, blown away at how everything had just lined up and unfolded.

Each time I met with Terri, she gave me homework to do. I would go home and do exercises that opened my mind up to the many aspects of the spiritual world. She helped me build a spiritual relationship with my father and God, and every week I began feeling better and better.

During our sessions, I had once informed Terri of how much it upset me that my dad's grave still didn't have a tombstone. Terri encouraged me to lead the change. I did. And soon after, my mom, auntie and I put together enough money to place a beautiful stone in his honor. Years later, I sent Terri a photo of the tombstone she had inspired me to have put up. She was thrilled to have been a part of this journey.

"Before our next session, I'd like you to get a piece of paper and write down all of the reasons you are angry and upset with your dad," Terri asked me one day.

"But, I'm not angry at him. He had no control over the situation, so it's not really *his* fault," I said.

Terri smiled at me and said, "Just try, write whatever comes to you."

Back at home, I struggled to get my feelings out on paper. But once I got the first emotion down, the rest came pouring out. To my surprise, I came back to our next session with two double-sided pages of things I was angry at him about:

Why did you have to walk us to school? Didn't you know it caused me to get bullied? Why didn't you teach me how to ride a bike? Why did you leave us? Why didn't you look after your health better? Why didn't you fight harder for your family? How could you leave mom all alone? Could you have drank less... quit smoking... anything...to not have had a stroke?

Terri had me go to his grave, read the list to him as if he was standing in front of me, and then burn the papers. This liberated me from the anger I held on to and gave me the greatest sense of relief and letting go.

Piece by piece, we broke down my pain: the guilt, sorrow, regret and blame. After three months, Terri told me I no longer needed to see her anymore. I was sad because I enjoyed our sessions immensely; Terri had become a friend to me. But at the same time, I felt happiness and gratitude that we had made it here.

ONE LAST STEP...

The morning after my final session with Terri, I ran into our room, where Dan was just waking up.

"I want to take you somewhere!" I said to Dan.

"OK, you seem happy," he laughed. "Where are we going?"

"Not telling, it's my turn to take you to an unknown location. Get ready! I'll meet you in the car!"

"Who has this much energy first thing in the morning?!" he joked.

"Me!" I echoed from the hallway.

It was the final thing Terri had asked me to do on our very last session. I was ready to finally stand at my dad's grave with another person.

Dan had no idea where I was taking him, but he agreed to come along.

As we got in the car, I left no gaps in my small talk to avoid the obvious questions. I could almost hear Dan's mind trying to guess as we drove along the main road, headed northwest towards the cemetery.

"I know where we're going," he said softly. I could tell he had worked it out by his tone.

"Where?" I asked to be sure, and to avoid accidentally confirming he was correct.

"The cemetery?" he asked.

"Yep, it's time," I replied. "I'm scared but I'm ready!"

"You got this," Dan declared confidently, raising a fist in the air.

As we stepped out of the car, my stomach was doing backflips. I could barely deal with coming here on my own, not to mention bringing someone else. At this point I had only just begun to build my spiritual relationship with my father. I worried if this was the right decision.

We stood in front of the dark gray marble tombstone. It was now engraved with gold letters, assembling words that perfectly mirrored how I felt— love. The breeze was smooth and my fears were gone. I placed a bunch of white roses into the vase cemented in the center.

Dan hugged me and kissed my forehead. "He's proud of you, Jules."

"I hope so," I replied as tears of joy slowly started to form and fill my eyes.

We stood in silence for a while, Dan's arm wrapped around my shoulder, and my head leaned securely on his. I embraced the moment; it was utterly perfect and still. God showed me tranquility that day.

Dan said a prayer, then looked back up at the grave.

"Rest in paradise, dad," he said softly.

I didn't say a word, but this moment meant the world to me. Dan was there for me like no one had ever been before. He helped me overcome this, and he helped me on the journey leading up to this day. I was certain in my belief that Dan would be in my life forever. No matter the challenge, we could always count on each other.

Lessons

SPIRITUALITY PROVIDES GUIDANCE AND INNER PEACE

"Mantra = Freeing the mind.
To transcend pain, you must first experience it"
—*Robin Sharma,* The Monk Who Sold His Ferrari

Life is about our questions. The questions that we ask, and the ones we are given. But it takes life experience to formulate a good question, and if you haven't dealt with enough problems, then there cannot be any solutions coming.

The connection I had with Simon and his mother inspired a breaking point, which launched a desire to create spiritual beliefs. It caused me to ask and seek answers. Open-mindedness was the only choice I had. Otherwise, I would not have listened to my inner voice and connected to a higher power. It wasn't easy, yet it was the right time in my life. I had to be fully where I was, completely accept myself and allow space for the closure that I was seeking.

When Dan shared his belief and faith with me, he introduced me to a totally new understanding of spirituality—where there was a greater being out there, something bigger than myself and what I perceive. Once I was open to receive, Terri came along and helped me complete the process of my healing: coming to accept the event that impacted my life so greatly.

These were the foundational moments that inspired my search for fulfilment in the Spiritual area of life. Later, I had to define what that meant to me and put in place a set of actions to incorporate my new beliefs into my daily life.

I started with the 10 minutes of silence that Bernard suggested on my rock bottom day. The combination of the Intellectual and Spiritual lessons that I learned through books, seminars and other spiritual and religious teachings, created the practices I use to align myself today.

Connection is alignment with your inner self, God, The Universe or (insert your own label here).

Fulfilment in the Spiritual area of life is a prerequisite for Best Life-ing, because whatever material successes we achieve on the outside, makes no difference if we do not have stillness within.

Anger is a normal part of our experience, and there's no reason to be ashamed of this emotion, but holding on to it is pointless. It only hurts you, the person feeling it. Our goal must be to release this feeling as quickly as possible.

If you regularly see the person you're angry with, resolve the situation by using the "Pineapple or no pineapple" method described in Chapter 2. However, what do you do if the person you're angry with is no longer around?

Terri's method of writing down all of the reasons you feel anger (even if you aren't aware of your anger) is one that can help you heal. Write it all down, find an appropriate place and release it by burning your anger.

As you begin to feel a sense of resolution, identify your spiritual connection or faith, or begin to search for it.

If you know your faith, how do *you* connect with it? Do you make time for it regularly or could this be improved?

If you haven't found your faith yet, don't worry. It's not a problem. Start with the same simple 10 minutes of silence every day. Even if you never identified with one of society's mainstream religions, you can still find the same clarity and focus from this habit.

HOW TO START A SIMPLE MEDITATION PRACTICE

When you make room in your life for silence, you simply give your mind a break—freeing it from thought. Our minds are always on the go. Everywhere we look, something or someone is competing for our attention, which we often give without even realizing it. For example, how many times a day do you find yourself being distracted by notifications on your phone?

We are constantly bombarded with other people's messages, belief systems and ideas for our life, which can influence our beliefs without us even knowing it. We then function on autopilot in accordance with these beliefs; our minds completely control us.

No wonder we feel stressed, lost or overwhelmed so often! This is why it is important to create habits that consciously allow our minds some quiet.

There is a considerable amount of information and research on this subject, the benefits and how to apply it in our everyday lives. Yet most people I speak with do not take *any* time for silence. Why?

The most common answer I receive is fear of failure or trying something new. People don't like to meditate because, at first, they can't get settled, their mind is overloaded with thoughts and they think they are doing it wrong. There is no wrong way to meditate; the goal is to rest the mind. The huge amount of thoughts coming at you are the exact thing you want to practice on—the thoughts are what you are trying to get a break from.

People often say to me that they can't stop their thoughts, because their mind is too scattered. Or every time they try, they can't stop the thoughts. This is completely normal. In the beginning, I couldn't slow down my racing mind even for a moment. But this is part of the process. Your mind will try to convince you that you're doing it wrong, but don't believe it. This is just another thought that will pass.

You can't get it wrong; there is no such thing. Like anything, with practice you will get better at it and find the ability to acknowledge each thought, and then release each thought. Improving our inner stillness, deepens our peace; and this results in how we respond to the outer world.

The easiest way to start a meditation practice is to find a quiet and comfortable place, close your eyes and count your breath. There are also plenty of guided meditations on YouTube to help you get started.

"How's your meditation going?" Bernard asked. It had only been a couple of weeks since I had started.

"It's okay, not the best. I can't seem to stop thinking, there's just so much going on in my head," I replied. "Plus the other day, I totally screwed up and fell asleep."

"There's no such thing as getting it wrong," he laughed. "The whole point is to see the thought, and then get rid of it by going back to your breathing. That's all you're doing over and over. Eventually, you get better and the thoughts become fewer and farther apart."

"But I don't feel like I'm getting anywhere with it, I have been doing it every day for a week."

"Could you learn the guitar or piano in a week? Another language? Or what about a new sport?"

"No, of course not," I laughed.

"Then be patient with yourself. It takes time. Meditation is a skill that needs to be learned and practiced like any other!"

Give your mind a break often, at least once a day. Take at least 10 minutes per day for the next 30 days and notice the difference in how you feel. Remember to be patient—you will get better at it.

GETTING OVER GRIEF

Our next focus will be on dealing with the grief of a loved one who has passed, and creating a spiritual connection with this person.

Terri taught me that there are seven stages of grief. To heal and come to acceptance with a loss, we must progress through each of them. No two individuals move through the grieving process in the same way. The stages can sometimes be simultaneous or can occur in different orders.

Shock or denial is usually the first stage. Shock is the body's way to provide emotional protection from being overwhelmed all at once. Denial about the situation or your emotions around it is often a common way your brain begins to process the traumatic event.

Soon pain and guilt take over. This makes you feel the heavy heartbreak of your loss, as well as guilt or regret for the things you did or didn't do. Understanding and allowing yourself to fully experience this pain is important, and being mindful of this can prevent you seeking an emotional escape. For example, drugs or alcohol.

You may soon find yourself blaming other people or even the world, for being unfair. You may begin to bargain with God or The Universe out of desperation, saying things like, "I will do anything if you just bring her back." This is natural in the anger and bargaining stage.

Eventually the true magnitude of your loss kicks in. This comes with feelings of pain, depression and loneliness. You may begin to put a lot of focus on memories from the past, feel a sense of emptiness or purposely isolate yourself.

As you slowly adjust and begin to pay more attention to your new life without your loved one, an upward turn begins. Things may not feel great, but time passes, life becomes more normal the way it is and you find ways to get reorganized, cope and focus your attention on new areas or projects.

As you begin to regain control and become more functional, you find yourself seeking more realistic solutions to practical and financial problems. You then start to reestablish yourself and work through.

In the last stage of grief, you begin to accept and deal with the reality of the situation. Acceptance doesn't equate to instant happiness, but you find a way forward once you accept and appreciate the experience for what it was with your loved one's presence. Eventually, you can connect with your loved one on a spiritual level. Some people do this by speaking to them during meditation. Others may feel their presence and guidance in moments of surrender, just like when I was guided to my dad's grave at the cemetery.

Building a spiritual relationship with a loved one is found by seeking out a space to connect and tune in enough to experience their presence.

When undesirable things happen and we truly accept them, we understand there is a place and purpose for them to have existed. We find peace within ourselves, and we create a grateful memory of that experience and how it impacted our life.

When we truly move on, our search for answers and reason diminishes, and our faith takes the space of that empty hole. This can only be achieved by bringing yourself into the present moment.

Eckhart Tolle teaches that time is an illusion. Only the present moment holds the key to liberation because nothing can ever happen in the "past" or the "future." Life always happens in the "now"—the past is just a memory activated in the now, and the future is an imagined scenario created in the now.

The best way to measure your success is by the level of peace you feel within. Ask yourself, "Do I feel good, calm and happy at this very moment?" Each moment of good feelings transfers to the next, as does each moment of not-so-good feelings.

Diary Entry

September 4th, 2018 – Rock City, Georgia

IT ALL STARTS IN THE MIND

Everything was seemingly perfect. Work was going well. I was doing big and small speaking gigs to groups of 30 or sometimes even 900 people at a time, teaching mindset, motivation and emotional intelligence. Every day I woke up thinking, *"This is so incredible."*

I never imagined that this experience would actually occur in my life—the irony is, I had to have imagined it. Truth be told, I once didn't know how to imagine. I didn't believe the law of attraction was real, that thoughts become reality and that you really can control what you attract into your experience.

I remember it was hard to be "happy" when everything felt "wrong" and "unfair." I hid behind the victim mentality label so faithfully. Although I was learning that it was all about mindset and perception, it still seemed extremely difficult to gain control of all of these endless thoughts running through my mind—especially the negative ones, which can have an overwhelming, compounding effect that can quickly send you into a depression.

I remember feeling disappointed when my positive thinking techniques didn't work or I didn't get the things I wanted right away. But every acknowledgement of what I didn't have, was the exact reason I didn't have it. See, that's how the whole "law of attraction" works: what we focus on is what we get more of. So nothing changed until I stopped telling myself the story that was, and started to tell myself the story I wanted.

Then, I broke my right arm. I fell off a hoverboard. Life without my right arm was devastating. Aside from the costs incurred from not having insurance in America, I was no longer able to work efficiently, write or even sign the bill at a restaurant. The pain was excruciating, and mentally, it brought me to a low place. I was on such a roll. Why did this have to happen?

My life changed when I decided to look at things differently. It's easy to complain and give up when life doesn't go our way, but that's just it—each difficulty is simply challenging how much you actually want the things that you say you want!

All of the basic things that I took for granted in my previous life became apparent. I had to completely start over. And very quickly, I felt worry and stress again. I became consumed by these negative emotions and stopped making time for myself and any form of alignment. Worry, worry, worry! Almost everything I had learned went out the window under pressure.

The only way out was from within.

Alignment and inner stillness is the first priority, especially when times are stressful. When I centered myself and silenced my mind, I could focus on each task in front of me without additional commentary about how hard it would be, risks and fears of failure. Once I got my mind right, it became much easier to handle anything.

This made me realize the benefits of my situation and served as a wonderful reminder that I have no complaints. It forced me to delegate better in my business (which has been more productive anyway); I've been able to catch up on things that I've wanted to do, passion projects and some much needed rest. And best of all, seeing the unbelievable kindness from my friends, family and even strangers, who have been helping during their own busy days and without personal gain, has been uplifting.

Eventually, things just started falling into place. This happened not because of one specific thing, but lots of different actions that eventually landed me exactly where I wanted to be geographically, financially and mentally. But it all started in the mind. I first envisioned my ideal future and got aligned with it. Then my dream began to manifest itself in real life.

KEY POINTS:

1. There is great benefit in finding your spiritual connection or faith.

2. Release your anger. Grab a blank sheet of paper and write down all of the reasons or angry feelings you have towards someone. Find a safe and private place, and then read those statements aloud. Burn the paper, be present and pay close attention to your feelings of anger as the paper burns.

3. Create gaps in the mind, learn to meditate or take time for silence. Get present in the moment.

4. Be patient with yourself; you will improve. And as anything else, meditation is a skill that needs to be learned and practiced.

5. A spiritual relationship with deceased loved ones is possible. Build yours with someone who has passed.

ACTION STEPS:

1. Release any anger toward any person or circumstance. Complete the exercise described in Key Point 2 above.

2. Take 10 minutes of silence per day for the next 30 days, no matter what—no excuses! This is a very important part of Best Life-ing. We all have 10 minutes. Make it happen.

Chapter Five

TABLE FOR FOUR

AREA OF LIFE 4/7: VOCATIONAL

I could feel the progress I was making. It energized me. My fulfillment in the Relational, Intellectual and Spiritual areas of life had heightened. I was getting along better with my mom and had a newfound spiritual relationship with my dad. I had attended seminars and enjoyed researching and learning more about spirituality. In moments of weakness, I relied on practices that I learned from Terri to find strength. Though my life was improving, I still had a long way to go. This progress was only almost half of what it takes to be truly Best Life-ing.

I took work very seriously and was soon promoted to lead my own restaurant, located in the international airport. It was exciting at first, and I enjoyed the challenge of it.

When I got promoted, Bernard and I started to spend more time together. He mentored me through the whole process of transitioning into my new role.

However, after a few months, I realized that I didn't enjoy being the boss. Enforcing policies, stressing about everything and performance management were not enjoyable for me. I felt that I couldn't be and express myself in this role.

To make matters worse, a combination of work and home-related problems were becoming stressful. Financial issues I had created, and being on call 24/7 for work had taken its toll on me. Dan was going through some major family and financial problems of his own, and he was constantly very unhappy.

Dan's motivation and presence in almost all situations was declining; he had no drive and wasn't interested in seeking help. It reminded me of myself not too long before. My instinct was to support him as he went through this, but instead, I unintentionally became the enabler. I began to spend a lot of time thinking about how I could make him happy or lift his mood. I'd bring his favorite food home every night or cook dinners, I'd speak about positive things and encourage him to go back to work. I'd plan date nights at the movies or restaurants, bring home sweet surprises and always tried to be in an uplifting mood, but nothing was working.

I had accumulated a large debt at this point. The banks called often to chase missed repayments, but I was paying all of Dan and my expenses. He wasn't coping well in his circumstances and he didn't have a source of income.

The bills were flowing in uncontrollably: food, rent, gas, electricity, cable and Internet. I couldn't keep up, maxing out all of my credit cards. On top of this, we often ate out and drank, plus we owed over $7,000 in parking fines. I needed to get another job just to keep up.

I knew Dan was going through a lot and he was always there for me when I needed him, so I wanted to do the same and stand by his side. I was afraid to ask him to help pay for our expenses because I didn't want to add to his stress. So I started working a second job at a bar near our apartment.

I hoped that when he saw me work so hard at two jobs, he would feel encouraged to get out there and work also, if not for himself, at least to help me help us. That didn't happen though. I just became more and more exhausted.

Each morning, a 5 a.m. start would tear me out of bed. I would work on my feet all day and regularly come home around two in the morning. The exhaustion and lack of sleep were killing me, and my temper became a short fuse.

Dan's sadness and depression soon turned to arguments. I started to completely lose sight of who I was, and reacted to situations purely on the emotion I felt at that moment. I couldn't help him. And after a full year, his slump had emptied the last of my energy.

MY CIRCLE OF LIMITING BELIEFS

Leaving the house helped me escape my problems; it took my mind off of what I felt at home. I started to spend a few nights a week sleeping over at Lisa's house.

"I don't know why you haven't just kicked him out already," Lisa said, pouring the last drops of Merlot into her glass.

"I can't do that, Lisa, you know how supportive he was when I really needed it," I explained.

"Yeah, well people change and he's using you!" she commanded. "Get rid of him."

Kicking Dan out was not an option, so I changed the subject. The truth is, I felt incredibly uncomfortable talking about Dan, with Lisa. Maybe because of how strongly she felt about him and that I didn't want our conversation to escalate into an argument. Or maybe because deep down I knew she was right, and I wasn't ready to accept it.

"OK, Lisa, forget about Dan. I came here to get my mind off it all," I said. "On a more positive note, there's a couple of things I've been thinking about a lot lately, and I seriously want to do them."

"Like what?" Lisa asked. I could sense the eye roll without looking at her. It was in her tone.

"I want to eat healthier and maybe get a little bit fitter. I've been reading a bit about organic…"

"Julia, let's be real. First, eating healthy is bullshit. They put preservatives and hormones into everything, so even when you think you're eating healthy, you're not," she ranted. "They force you to buy all the organic bullshit, that's just a government conspiracy so that they can get more money off you."

"But," I tried to interrupt.

"Wait, I'm not done," she stopped me. "It's too expensive, how are *you* going to afford it? Rhetorical question—you're not! Besides, you're already dependent on the nasty shit they poison our food with, so you're never going to be able to stop." I didn't really want to agree with her, but her points seemed valid enough and her passion was convincing.

"OK, what about something for fitness. Do you want to do some type of exercise with me?"

"Yeah, I need to lose weight, but I'm fine just walking to the train station every morning," she replied. "Plus, if you want to join a gym or something, it's all pretentious assholes in there, and I hate being told what to do when I'm exercising. Anyway, if you do that, you're gonna walk in there looking like an idiot. You have no idea what you're doing in a gym. And do you really want big muscles like all those chicks that look like dudes?"

She laughed. My idea was completely idiotic to her. *"Maybe she is right,"* I thought. Her limiting beliefs were infusing into my subconscious. Like a cup of tea, the flavors would remain long after the tea bag is removed.

"The food you cook is fine," Lisa continued, "and if you go for a walk every now and then, you'll be fit. Don't waste your money."

"Yeah, I guess you're right....OK, next topic," I said, provoking her to talk about something else.

"Anyway, did you hear about the fight that Maddy and Chris had? I bet you they're gonna break up soon. He is a shit boyfriend anyway...she can do so much better!" Lisa preferred to talk about other people's problems, most likely to deflect the focus off her own.

That night, even though I probably had more drinks than I should have, I wasn't in the mood to stay over. On my way home, I turned up the music to mask my thoughts.

"Hey, Dan," I said as I walked in the apartment. He was smoking a joint.

"Hey, Jules, you want some?" he replied, reaching out his hand with the blazing stick.

"Sure," I sat down on the couch and took it from him. Inhale, exhale, problems gone.

Dan and I had been smoking every day for over a year. He stayed up late until I came home from work, and slept it off, half of the following day. When I smoked weed, it would make me forget all the problems around me, but the drug made me angry and paranoid when it wore off.

When I look back, I see that all that the weed did, was bring me into the present moment. That's why it felt that nothing was wrong. It would give me a break from thinking, and gave me stillness by creating gaps in my mind. This is the feeling that we are internally seeking, the silence and gaps strengthen our inner resilience and, in turn, how we respond to our outer experience.

"Dan, I want to get fitter," I began, now less concerned if I actually did. "You want to do some physical activities on the weekend?"

"Ha!" he laughed. "What, like the gym? I'm not hanging out with those douchebags."

"It doesn't have to be the gym," I replied. "Let's just go for a hike or something, get some air and nature?"

"Nah, I'm not into all that noise," he said. "Take one of your other mates…wait shh, this is the good bit of the show."

I could have taken another friend with me, I could have gone alone, but I didn't. It felt easier to just go with the flow. I felt that if no one else around me wanted to do it, maybe I was just being ridiculous.

The following day I was opening the mail while Dan sipped his coffee on the couch.

"Shit!" I yelled out.

"What up?" Dan lifted his face from his phone.

"I got done by another speed camera ticket. They're suspending my license!"

"You're so silly, kiddo, why don't you drive like a normal person…you know, under the speed limit!" he joked.

"It's not funny!" I snapped.

"I know. I'm just trying to make light of it," Dan said. "It sucks, but welcome to the train life."

"Arghhh, I hate everything!" I raged, storming out of the room.

At work I had a friend named Cassie. We had been close for a while and regularly met early at work to plan the day ahead. We sat outside in the airport's wind tunnel on a cold silver bench, savoring the warmth of our caramel lattes.

"Guess what happened?" I complained.

"What!? You won the lotto?…. We're outta here? Let's go! We don't need bags, we can buy new stuff—we're already at the airport anyway!" she laughed.

"Haha, I wish," I said, imagining it for a moment. "No, I'm losing my license."

"Let me guess, speeding again?" Cassie replied.

"Yeah."

"Well, you're an idiot! But welcome to train life!" she teased. I wasn't as annoyed when Cassie said it. Maybe I had already accepted the situation or had had the time to process it; or maybe I had grown resentful of Dan.

"How's everything with you?" I asked Cassie.

"Shit," she replied. "I can't deal with my psycho sister anymore, and there's not enough room in my mom's house. I need to find a place."

"Well, I have an extra room if you want? And I could use some help paying the rent," I offered.

"That's right, you've still got that drop-kick Dan mooching off you," she said.

"It's not like that, Cassie," I defended.

"Oh yeah? Then why don't you tell him to go get a job and pay rent like everyone else in this world?" she challenged.

"Because! He's going through some shit. You have no idea how it used to be, he's a good guy," I replied.

"He's a parasite!"

"Watch, when he gets through this, he'll go back to normal and everything will be better." This was my delusion, again escaping the present searching for happiness in the imagined future.

"Whatever, it's your life! And yes, I'll move in!" she said excitedly.

"Great! That's so exciting!" I exclaimed. "Crap, look at the time, we gotta get to work!"

The following week, Cassie filled my car with her suitcases and boxes to move into my place. Five laps later we were done moving everything from one house to the other. We dropped on the couch out of exhaustion. Dan was already sitting there.

"Ahhh, so glad that's over!" Cassie exhaled. "Lucky I didn't have that much stuff."

"Yeah, now we can relax!" I confirmed.

"Do you guys have any weed?" she asked.

"Sure do!" Dan replied.

"Sweet!" Cassie cheered.

The three of us living together wasn't inspiring. We became enablers for one another to do the least. Nourished with only Domino's pizza and smoking weed every day, we were glued to the couch. The lethargic effect of these habits removed all reason for aspiration and, now that Cassie had moved in, I didn't need a second job. So I quit working at the bar.

I was in a rut and soon we all were, but none of us were even remotely interested in digging ourselves out.

The trains were packed every morning in Sydney's cold, wet winter. I would board every day, hating every moment of the uncomfortable and squashy experience. The trains were unreliable, and by the end of the day, the last thing I wanted to do was catch the peak hour train ride home.

There was a bar upstairs from where I worked in the airport, so I would sit there and wind down until the rush hour finished. A couple of drinks every day turned into bottles very quickly. Eventually I would be drinking well after the peak rush hour and late into the night.

Dan used my car while my license was suspended. Sometimes he would pick me up, others he'd stay out late and ignore my calls. I suppressed these concerns with weed and entire bottles of wine.

A NEW OPPORTUNITY SPARKS A DREAM

"What was that all about?" Cassie asked one day as I walked into the office from the unplanned meeting my boss had arranged.

"She just offered me a new role in the RTO!" I replied.

The RTO stands for Registered Training Organization: a department in the head office of McDonald's Australia that provides training and nationally recognized qualifications to employees who complete the program. This was the program that I completed when I first started after leaving highschool—the program that engaged me and introduced me to my first taste of achievement.

"Oh wow, OK, so you're leaving?" Cassie confirmed.

"Yeah, I think I'm going to take the job. But don't worry, we're still going to see each other all the time at home!" I replied.

"Thank God I don't have to work with you anymore!" she laughed.

"Shut up, you'll miss me when I'm gone," I joked.

When I started in the RTO, I loved it instantly. The job was easy for me because it catered to my strengths, yet I was learning the technical aspects of training, compliance and building content.

The company put me through various courses, and I achieved my diploma of training and assessment in education. I was constantly learning new skills on the job and this got me excited for life again. I stopped smoking every day because I was inspired and focused; I didn't need it to get into the present moment, because I loved being there…well, at least for a little while.

The job was extremely rewarding for me. I worked closely with kids like myself, aged between 15-25 mostly, helping them achieve their Certificate II & III in retail.

Many of the young adults I mentored shared similar mentalities: they spoke of feeling lost in life, depressed or uninspired. They would usually start the course with me because they were required to, and with a "might as well" attitude. Many told me about their self-confidence issues. Some had trouble with language, literacy and numeracy, as well as their own limiting beliefs. I recognized their struggles all too well. Death, learning disabilities or toxic relationships were common themes in our conversations. And like me, they had often been judged for working at McDonald's and scrutinized for not being "good enough."

I knew they *were* good enough; they simply had difficulties and challenges just like everyone else. We all need someone to believe in us, and we need to believe in ourselves. I wanted to help them see this, like my boss once did for me, because nothing builds confidence and self-esteem like accomplishment.

Many of my students had never achieved any type of qualification before, and it would take most of the students anywhere from six months to two years to complete their qualification. During this time, I worked with them side by side through the whole process. I got to know the kids well. I knew their troubles, their fears and their stories. I shared mine to let them know they were not alone.

With each module completion, the students' confidence grew. It wasn't just a job to me; I was personally invested in seeing my students succeed.

A common fear many of my students shared was that they were petrified of bookwork. Ava was one of them. She was a sweet, shy 14-year-old girl, petite and reserved. She was so nervous during her first assessment that we had to reschedule when she broke down in tears halfway through.

Ava couldn't read or write well, but she was good at retaining information from the skills she learned hands on. What's more, her skills at demonstrating the assessment's practical components were outstanding. While I could conduct a verbal assessment and do the reading and writing for her, the issue was in her fear. She was so overwhelmed by it that even though she was on track to pass the assessment, she gave up. When she came back the second time, I tried again with a different method.

"Hi Ava, how are you?" I greeted her.

"I'm OK," she said softly.

"OK, good. Now, I'm not going to ask you how you feel about your assessment this time, because I don't even want you to think about it," I said. "Forget what happened last time and tell me, what's the highlight of your week so far?"

"My sister took me to a really nice restaurant," Ava replied, smiling as she began to picture the moment.

"Nice, what did you order from the menu?" I continued.

"I had the grilled chicken and chips," she replied.

I continued to ask her a series of questions, which gave me enough information to link the assessment questions to her personal experiences.

"OK, Ava, now let's forget about the assessment and pretend we are just continuing our conversation, OK?" I said.

"OK," she replied, though I could see her nerves re-emerging.

"Don't be nervous, we're just talking like normal," I assured her. "The first question is about handwashing, so just tell me about that. When you come into work, how do you normally wash your hands?"

"Well, I put them under the water...oh my gosh...I don't know!" she panicked.

"Come on, Ava, I know you know this. Forget about the assessment. Just remind me how to wash my hands, I forgot," I said.

"OK," she giggled, and then exhaled. "OK, first wet them, then add the soap..."

"What's the soap called again?" I asked.

"Anti...micro...bacterial handwash!" she said proudly.

"Very good, and what do you do with it?"

"You put it all the way up to your elbows and rub it in for 30 seconds," she replied, "and then you wash it off and dry it."

"Can I just dry my hands on my apron or something?" I joked.

"No! You have to use the hand towels or the air dryer!" she laughed.

"See, this is easy, right?"

"Yeah, it's actually fun!" she giggled.

"OK, the next question is about temperature. Remember the chicken they gave you at the restaurant with your sister? What temperature did it have to be before it went on your plate?" I asked.

"Easy, 74 degrees celsius!" she answered.

Ava's problem was not that she didn't have the knowledge, it was that her past experiences had given her a paralyzing fear of examinations.

"I can't believe I passed it!" she celebrated after I announced her result.

"I knew you would!" I replied. "See, nothing to worry about."

"Thank you so much for helping me."

"I didn't do anything, it was all you," I smiled. "Well done, I'm proud of you."

I had more purpose in this role than I ever did as a restaurant manager. These kids made me realize that there was nothing more rewarding than helping others. We grew together, because helping people makes you grow just as much as they do in the process.

12 months later Ava completed her traineeship. She was so lively that day; she believed she could achieve anything now and this was so delightful for me to watch.

"Miss Julia," Ava said as we sat beside each other signing off the last of her completion paperwork.

"You don't need to call me that," I laughed.

"Well, you're the best teacher I've had, so I want to," she said.

"Oh the irony," I thought.

If only I knew this moment was coming 10 years ago when I dropped out, I wouldn't have wasted so much time being upset about it all.

"Thank you, Ava, that means a lot to me," I replied.

"Will you come to my graduation?" Ava asked.

"Absolutely! I can't wait to see you on that stage with the crowd cheering."

"Me too, it's the first time I've ever graduated anything!" she announced proudly.

What a successful day. Satisfaction filled my body and my entire soul was smiling. I felt all sorts of wonderful sensations: love, joy, wisdom and purity, to name a few. Everything seemed like it was coming together.

"This is what I want to do forever!" I thought to myself as I bounced back to my car.

ONE STEP FORWARD, TWO STEPS BACK

That evening, I had dinner plans with Lisa, and she reserved us a table at a Thai restaurant in the city. The drive there was phenomenal; I was thinking about all of the wonderful things I could do and be in the future. I was forming my dreams!

"Hey Lisa!" I spotted her sitting at a large table alone. "What's with the extra seats and big table, this place is packed."

"Hey," Lisa replied as I walked up to the table. "I got us a table for four because this place is kind of squashy."

Lisa was being a bit dramatic. The tables were fine. But I was used to it; she was always a bit high maintenance like that.

"Aren't they going to say something when no one else comes?" I laughed.

"Yeah, we'll just say they're running late or some shit," she explained.

"Lisa, I had the best day today!" I announced excitedly.

"Oh yeah, why's that?" she asked, dipping a rice paper roll into the sticky sauce beside it. "Try one of these."

"It was just a really great day at work, my new job is so rewarding, I love it!"

"That's good, how are your new bosses and the team?" she continued.

"They're really great, lovely people, but I work mainly on the road, so I don't really see them that much," I said.

"Even better," Lisa replied. "You can do whatever you want."

"That's it, Lisa! Today one of my students inspired me so much, I know what I want to do now!" I couldn't contain my excitement. I really wanted to share the feeling with Lisa, and the world!

"A kid inspired you?" she clarified sarcastically while trying to be funny. "Wait, I mean one of your *dropout* kids inspired you, oh jesus…haven't you been one of those already?"

Lisa *was* joking around at that point. My friends and I had a strange sense of humor where we often made jokes that put each other down.

"That's exactly why I think it's perfect. I understand what they're going through and I really think that I can help," I replied.

"OK, so what is it that you want to do?" she asked seriously now.

"I don't know exactly," I began. "I love writing, so maybe I will put down everything that I have learned into a book. Then I could do my own classes. And I know it's going to sound crazy, but I could be a speaker one day and try to help lots of people with all the lessons that I've learned. Then they won't have to make the same mistakes that I went through!"

"OK seriously, Julia, did you forget to take your meds this morning?" she was joking about the meds, but serious about the message of the joke.

"Lisa, I'm serious," I replied.

"That's what I'm worried about, you're setting yourself up for disappointment," she said. "I've been your friend the longest. Maybe your other friends don't care, but I don't want to see you go through all of that just to get disappointed."

I listened to what she had to say.

"That sounds like a bunch of hippy garbage," she continued. "No offense, but let's be realistic. Why would anyone read your book or listen to you? What experience have you got?"

"I just told you," I defended. "I've been through it. I really feel like I could help."

"Yes, but a sad story is one thing," she explained. "Who's going to read a book from a 25-year-old who works at McDonald's? Like it's a good job and all, but you gotta go to university and do something amazing…you know, so people will respect you."

"Maybe I am being ridiculous, she's probably right. Who would want to listen to what I've got to say?" I thought to myself.

"Julia, life is bullshit," she said surely. "The only thing good is to look forward to a holiday. You know that, you've been through so much."

"There has to be more, Lisa," I interrupted.

"I'm sorry, but there really isn't," she argued. "Apart from holidays, we are just slaving away at work, paying bills and doing what we need to to get by. Stop wasting your time on this hippy shit, and plan a holiday so you have something to look forward to. That's a good life."

Lisa was my oldest friend, and she didn't believe in me. Could I have possibly believed in myself without her? Yes, but I was afraid to lose her in doing it. I was also afraid that she was right. What if I did fail? I didn't want to hear "I told you so."

"I'm not being mean, I'm just trying to be a good friend," Lisa would justify.

It wasn't her fault; a dream like that to Lisa was truly impossible in her mind. They were just her limiting beliefs, and she projected them onto me, in an attempt to protect me. Her intentions were good. But her approach wasn't the best for either of us.

If you have a friend who doesn't believe in you, I recommend evaluating how much time you spend with that person. Remember, the people that try to bring you down (intentionally or not) must be standing lower than you in the first place.

Truth be told, Lisa wasn't the only negative influence in my life. I hadn't done anything really impressive, but that didn't mean it was too late to start (unless I believed it).

Unfortunately, the people we surround ourselves with have a big influence on our behavior and decisions. I have made many bad choices because of the community I surrounded myself with, but I'll save that for the next chapter.

"Excuse me, do you have two more people still coming?" the Thai waitress asked.

"Oh, no, sorry, they cancelled," Lisa replied.

On the drive home from dinner, my mood was the complete opposite from the drive on the way there. I walked into the apartment where Cassie and Dan sat on the couch laughing.

"Heyyyy! She's home," Cassie cheered. "Surprise, we've got Domino's pizza! You want some?"

"No," I replied.

"Bad day, kiddo?" Dan handed me a joint. "Here, smoke some of this."

"Guys, I don't want to just eat shitty Domino's pizza and smoke weed all the time!" I complained.

"Yep, definitely a bad day," Cassie turned and said to Dan. She then looked back at me, "But we've got ranch sauce to make it better!"

They both giggled. I softened up.

"What's up?" Dan said.

"I actually had a great day, like the best day at work today," I said. "But then I went to dinner with Lisa and she killed my entire mood...or maybe I just don't like hearing the truth."

"That's the only reason she doesn't want pizza, she had dinner already," Cassie joked to Dan again.

"Cassie, I'm being serious," I said.

"Sorry! I'm just trying to cheer you up," Cassie replied. "OK seriously, so you had a great day and then Lisa pissed you off. What happened?"

"She didn't piss me off. She just doesn't believe in me," I said.

"We believe in you, Juju. You're gonna take over the world some day!" Dan cheered.

"Yeah, the whole wide world! Here..." Cassie laughed as she passed me the joint. "What did Lisa not believe you about?"

"No, I said believe *in me*. Forget it," I said, taking a big inhale of the joint. They were both too high to talk to anyway.

The next morning, Cassie came over to me on the balcony and sat down. Dan was still asleep.

"Hey, I'm sure he's going to tell you anyway," she whispered. "But I was talking to Dan last night and he said he's going back to work in the night clubs. You should speak to him about throwing in some rent..."

"Oh really?" I replied. "Nice how he told you before me. OK, so what should I say to him?"

"How about... bitch better have my money!" she sang the Rihanna hit.

"Cassie!"

"OK, OK...I don't know, just ask him. Blame it on me or some shit," she whispered.

Later that day I spoke to Dan, and he agreed to pay rent. But working in clubs brought a wave of destruction with it—he now stayed out all night from Thursday to Monday. If he came home at 9 a.m., it was an early bender, and I would knock back some drinks with him. This habit took a toll on both of our bodies, and soon it greatly affected our relationship.

Before I knew it, Cassie and I were out with Dan almost every weekend. We would party into the next morning, take drugs, drink ridiculous amounts of alcohol and waste our days being hungover.

I stopped caring about dreams, my health or anything that should have mattered. The only agenda was to work Monday to Friday and get an outfit for partying on the weekend.

AN INSPIRATIONAL INFLUENCE

"I haven't seen Bernard in a while," I thought to myself as I got in the car one day after work. I was planning to drive home and then eat at the local sports bar because it was easier. I picked up my phone to call Bernard.

"Hey, what are you doing tonight? Want to have dinner?" I offered.

"Sure, I can do that," Bernard replied. "Where do you want to go?"

"Just the sports bar is fine. I feel like staying local," I replied.

"OK, I can be there at 6:30?"

"Yep, works for me, see you then."

Bernard was one of the only people I could have a thought-provoking conversation with. He challenged me and always encouraged me to dream.

He'd spend countless hours talking to me and trying to help me on a subject. Which was great. I would leave our conversations feeling inspired. The issue was I'd then go back into my core circle of friends, who didn't know this world of success. I would get a taste, but it was just so much easier to fall back into my old ways than to work hard for what I wanted. I had no idea what I was missing.

When I was with Bernard, I wanted to change. He made me want to achieve success, and even made it seem possible. When I was with all my other friends, I would drink until I collapsed.

"Two wines and two steaks again?" the waiter offered, at our usual restaurant hangout.

"Yes, mine with just chips please, no salad," Bernard requested before turning to me. "OK, so what's been happening?"

"Eh, same old. Just always tired," I replied.

"How's work going?"

"It's good, oh by the way, I decided I don't want to be the CEO anymore."

"And why is that?" Bernard asked.

"I don't like bossing people around. And I have a better idea, a new dream!" I said excitedly.

"Well that's good, because I don't think you would have become the CEO."

"What's that supposed to mean, Bernard?"

"I told you, to be the CEO you need to have discipline and you will need to make sacrifices. You do not like discipline and you definitely aren't making any sacrifices right now!" Bernard laughed out loud as he finished his sentence.

"Yeah, that's true," I laughed with him.

"What is your new dream, Julia?"

"To be honest, it might sound stupid, but I want to be a motivational speaker," I replied instantly. "I really love writing, too, so I want to put together everything I've learned and help people like me that are going through hard times."

"Well, what do you need to be able to do that?" Bernard replied.

"I don't know. Time, money," I said as my tone slightly deflated. "Besides, who's going to listen to me?"

"Yes," Bernard began. "This is all true and I'm going to tell you how it works. The first step is to aspire. You've done that, very good, but you also need to get that vision clear on exactly what you want. The second step is to absorb, you need to absorb lots of information to learn and grow yourself. You are a smart girl but you still have a lot to learn. The third step is to apply what you learn, because you can read a million books and go to a million seminars, but if you don't apply what you learn, there is no point. And the final step is to maintain attention. This is the one that I feel you, Julia, will struggle with."

"Why? I can pay attention," I said.

"Yes, you can pay attention," Bernard replied. "But I am telling you that you have to *maintain* attention. This means when your friends invite you to go party, you stay home and write your book. This means when people go on a holiday, you say 'no.' You save your money and invest it into learning how to become a great speaker."

"Are you serious? I can't enjoy life and go on holidays?" I reacted.

"If you want your dream, there is going to be a price. Everything has a price," Bernard said.

I nodded. I knew he was right.

"And one more thing," Bernard added. "If you want to be successful, we need to break down some of those limiting beliefs."

"What limiting beliefs? I don't have any," I said.

"As I said, Julia, you are a smart girl but you always seem to question yourself and mention all the things you can't do."

"I don't mean it like *that*," I assured.

"I think you do. When you say you haven't got time, money or whatever, you believe your excuse. When you ask questions like, 'who is going to listen to me speak?' you confirm that you do not believe in yourself."

The following week, I somehow convinced Lisa to attend a motivational seminar with me. I sat next to her, having such a great time. I felt so inspired and ready to change my life even more. After about 30 minutes into the 2-hour presentation, Lisa leaned over and whispered, "This is bullshit, I'm going to the bar."

Instinctively, I was about to follow her because this is what I would normally do, but this time I didn't want to. I was really enjoying myself, and I remembered what Bernard said: I would need to make a choice, sacrifice or pay a price. I would need to choose between my old ways or my dreams. And this time, I wanted my success more than I wanted "another drink at the bar."

You've probably heard the old saying, "You are the average of the top five people you surround yourself with." I was beginning to see how this principle played out in my own life.

"Sorry, I'll meet you there after," I whispered back.

I'm glad I stayed and finished that seminar, because the speaker recommended a book that has had a huge influence on my life: *The Law of Attraction* by Esther and Jerry Hicks. I later used the concepts in this book to dramatically alter my perspective.

After the seminar, I walked out of the large auditorium and headed over to Lisa at the bar.

"Hey, finally!" Lisa said. "I wanted to tell you, while you were in there, me and the girls were planning our next holiday. We're going to Hunter Valley vineyards this weekend. Are you gonna come?"

"Who's going?" I considered.

"Me, Kristy, Melanie, Tina... and you?" she questioned.

"I can't this weekend, Lisa, I already made plans," I answered.

"Come on, what plans? How am I gonna handle all those dramatic, high-maintenance girls without you?" she nagged.

"I don't know... but at least now you can book a table for four!"

Lessons

HOW TO DISCOVER YOUR VOCATION

A purposeful career is a huge part of Best Life-ing. We spend at least a quarter of our life at work, so it's no surprise that people who are unhappy, often aren't passionate about their job.

Before you can live your vocation, you need to figure out what it is. Trial and error may reveal it to you eventually, but I've also seen it make people give up on their dreams. So, how do you figure out your individual dream, niche, mission or calling? And then, how can you turn that into your vocation or career?

You may feel that you have no idea what your dream is, that it is impossible to achieve, or you may have forgotten how to dream. Too many let downs? That's alright, it is possible!

Determining your dream is not as difficult as you may think. Write a list of the things you are passionate about. What is it that you really love to do?

Ask yourself the question: *if I could do anything in this world, starting right now, and I know there is no possibility of failure, what would it be?* If money, time, knowledge or market competitiveness weren't an issue, what would you choose to do?

Your vocation will be the thing that you do best, is instinctive and feels like it requires no effort. You also want to make sure it's the right dream. Your dream is yours—not anyone else's. Your dream needs to align with who you are, not what somebody else thinks you should do.

THE PROBLEM WITH MOTIVATION

I want to make it clear to you, my dear reader, that your dream cannot be achieved through motivation. I know this from first hand experience after motivation repeatedly failed me.

Challenges and circumstances easily exhaust motivation. That's why you need to discover what inspires you; inspiration puts up a much bigger fight. So search deep inside to find what inspires you in your core. Your dream needs to be aligned with every inch of who *you* are, not what anyone else believes to be right.

Surrendering to other people's expectations and beliefs, is a sure way to procrastinate, hesitate and miss out on many opportunities.

Inspiration comes from within, while motivation relies on external forces. Motivation places the focus on the outcome of having something tangible; it pushes or persuades you to take action. Inspiration pulls you towards it.

Challenges will cross your path on the journey towards your dream. And achieving it will require sacrifices and discipline. Unfortunately, motivation won't help you when it gets hard. You need a big enough reason. You need a *why*.

To find a big enough reason, write down 105 reasons why this dream will improve your life and another 105 reasons for how it will help others. This isn't an easy task. But it will give you a big enough reason to triumph over challenges.

Why a strange number like 105? The first 20 will get you thinking, 50-75 becomes a challenge, 75-100 gets you really digging for reasons and 105 gives you a *why* that can elevate you to greater levels. Anything more is a bonus.

What this does is cause your brain to rewire its beliefs, visualize new possibilities and have a big enough reason to show up, get out of bed and achieve your new, bigger goals.

Once you know the dream, it's time to chase it—this can be frightening at first. But other people can and will benefit from you overcoming your fear, and the ripple effect that comes when you live out your dreams. It is not selfish to live your dream; actually, it would be more selfish to not do the work.

Find your dream, get a big enough reason and start living it now! That's not saying to quit your job and go jump right into your dream. Instead, take one small action towards your dream each day. This will result in 365 actions per year. That's huge. You'll be surprised how quickly progress happens through small actions.

CLARIFY YOUR DREAMS AND RELISH THE JOURNEY

Sometimes you're going to have to do what you don't want to do, until you can do what you love. Search for value in what you do. Do it with the highest integrity and see how it may link to your future vocation.

For example, I once had an office job where I had to constantly use Excel spreadsheets, which were unstimulating, to say the least. But linking this tedious task to how it could possibly assist me in my dream later on, made it agreeable. Excel is essential in my businesses today. I'm glad I put in the effort to master the application. This mindset can be applied to any tedious task. Link the task to your dream, and you will find more satisfaction in doing it.

Even your dream will become a job one day. There will be responsibilities that you don't enjoy doing, so even if the only value you get out of completing these tedious tasks is discipline, you're already winning. Take it easy on yourself. Slowly start to enjoy what you're doing on the journey to your dream.

On my 25th birthday, Bernard gave me a book titled *101 Dreams*. I flipped through the blank pages to discover that the stories were mine to write. Completing this journal has been incredibly helpful for me, and I believe a similar exercise can benefit you just as greatly.

Put your dreams in writing.

Not only does this help you get clear on what you want, but it's also fun to review at a later date. We often don't realize the magnitude of our accomplishments, until we look back to see how far we've come.

Success needs momentum, and one of the best ways to gain momentum is through accomplishment.

A wonderful family in New York taught me a valuable lesson. We met on a cruise in 2015, and we kept in touch via the internet until a few years later when they welcomed me into their home. The Moore family likes to celebrate everything. They would celebrate moments together, achievements small or large, events and even desires—just an idea could be a celebration, well before anything had come from it.

Celebrate your progress and every small win, celebrate the people you love and their achievements, celebrate everything and nothing. Life gives you so many things to celebrate. Don't get caught up in what's not done, and give yourself some credit for what is. You're doing fine!

COMMON HURDLES ON THE PATH TO YOUR DREAMS

Ultimately, all your stress and anxiety is caused by noticing where you stand, but wanting to stand somewhere else. It is normal to want more and think about the future, but we can only take action at this moment in time.

One sure way to demotivate yourself at any point, but especially when getting started, is to compare yourself to others who have achieved success, or are even slightly further along on the path to their dream. Know your position, appreciate it and get comfortable with being there; everybody starts there, and all of these success stories began in the same place where you are right now. You may have heard the phrase "it takes 10 years to become an overnight success." This saying means that *you* probably only heard of a successful person once he or she made it big, after 9 years and 364 days. Before then that person had a much smaller audience.

Scroll far down enough any influencers social media page, or search back to the YouTube song covers your favorite artist was doing when they were younger. Their overnight success was a very long, long night.

What's more, most successful people are willing to help, if you show that you value their time by taking action. Ask successful people for help, offer to buy them a coffee for their advice or just shoot them a message. While you may not always get a favorable response, you may be surprised how people genuinely want to help others. Be sure to show respect for their time by taking action or they won't be inclined to help you again.

This leads me onto failure. When you fail, which you will, don't be discouraged. Who cares! Every "no" is one step closer to the right "yes." An expression I once heard that has helped me overcome failure is, "some will, some won't, who cares, who's next." As in, some people will want to do, help or participate in your dreams, some people will not. Who cares, don't let it deter you, and who's next? Eventually someone will want to do, help or participate. But all of the "whys" behind the "nos" will show you how to get your "yes."

Fail, fail often, fail quickly, learn from it and move forward. It's not bad to fail, jump right in! By doing the things that scare you, you can squash any fear. If you're worried about what people will think, the reality is, no matter who you are or what your dream is, you can't escape criticism and judgment. There will always be naysayers. Just like my friend Lisa, they may even think they are protecting you from your dream, or they may not have

135

the capacity to fathom the possibility of your dream. You may have heard of these people as haters, critics or skeptics. They might refer to themselves as realists, often misusing this word.

But really, they are faultfinders because regardless of their intentions, they will find fault in your dream. They will point out your shortcomings, disadvantages or obstacles, rather than cheer you on. I believe that regardless of how unrealistic your dream seems, you owe it to yourself to at least try to achieve it.

It's very common for people to spend their entire life wanting something more and waiting for the right time to start living. But there is no way to live and love your life from the future. Get clear on this—the only time you can live your dream is right now. The only time you can start your dream is in the present. Your many small actions in the present moment will assemble your future.

And finally, how do you know when you've found your vocation?

When you feel the excitement to get up in the morning, you can't wait to start your work and you wrestle yourself to put it down at the end of a day—that's your dream.

Diary Entry

September 23rd, 2018 – Lagos, Portugal

REALITY BOOK

As I flip through the pages of my dream book (I wonder if it is more appropriate to call it a reality book these days), I reflect and appreciate all that has passed. I have so much gratitude for this moment.

Looking back, I see how much my belief in my capabilities has evolved. This moment serves as a reminder of how and why this progression has happened, as I sit on this simple rock, overlooking this magical city while the sun sets on another day.

Each dream is met with another, and each moment is full of surprises. Embracing these moments hasn't always been easy, but I'd do it all again in a heartbeat.

My work is my passion. I know this because even while I am here on this holiday, I can't stop my pen from meeting the page. Five years ago, I wrote in my dream book:

The Happiness Project: find my happy, help others find it sooner, write a book, start a company that inspires & motivates others, travel the world.

The experience of writing those words comes back to me each time I read them. I *wanted* them, but I didn't really believe that putting them in this dream book made any difference. Ah, if I could go back and speak to my past-self as the person I am today, I'd simply say, "Don't stress girl, you want it? Write it down and go be happy, everything you want is on its way."

137

KEY POINTS:

1. Your dream is yours, not anyone else's.

2. Make sure it's the right dream. You need a big enough *why* to get through the challenges that are ahead.

3. Get a dream book. Put your dreams on paper. Write, draw, cut and paste, whatever feels good. These small actions will help you commit and give you something tangible to look back on.

4. Sometimes you'll have to do things you don't want to before you can do what you love. Link what you're doing today to your dream.

5. Don't compare yourself to others. Don't worry about faultfinders.

6. Celebrate your small wins and fail fast and often.

ACTION STEPS:

1. Figure out your dream job/career/vocation.

2. Write, draw or cut and paste it into your dream book.

3. Write down at least 105 reasons why *you* want to achieve it. Write 105 reasons how it will impact others. You need a big enough *why* to push past the inevitable obstacles ahead. Creating this list may take a few days.

Chapter Six

FROSTY FLOORS

AREA OF LIFE 5/7: SOCIAL

I opened my eyes, but everything was still blurry. I felt the stony, wet floor tiles underneath my head and body as the sound of panic echoed from screaming voices. But I had no idea where I was or what was going on.

"She's waking up!"

As my vision focused, I realized there were two paramedics standing over my body, which was collapsed on the floor. Confused, I looked over to my left where I saw my heartbroken mother and two of my friends. I realized there was water all over me, and a huge, throbbing lump on the right side of my head.

I wondered if I was still dreaming, though something told me I wasn't. How was it possible that I had no recollection of how I got here?

12 HOURS EARLIER

"Good Morning!" Cassie yelled, when she saw I had finally rolled out of bed. "Happy Birthday!"

It was Saturday afternoon around midday.

"Thank you!" I replied, feeling hungover. "Oh shit, my head is spinning."

My splitting headache and throbbing body weren't a result of last night's special celebration. Hangovers were my norm. Even though Bernard made big efforts to help me make good decisions, I spent more time with Cassie and Dan. Dan was always partying, and I wanted to join in; Cassie would usually agree and off we went! I had to. I hated to hear stories of things that I missed out on.

Saying I felt hungover is an understatement. Most days I felt like I got hit by a bus and reversed back over; however, since today was my birthday, I had to get it together, rather than sleep through the day until my next drink. I was going to have a big party tonight.

Arranging events always maxed out my stress levels, and tonight was especially important to me. I wanted to make sure everyone had a great time, and everything had to be perfect. I put a lot of pressure on myself to make sure that nothing would go wrong.

I dressed in a beautiful, long purple gown, enhanced with floral prints and skirt puffs at the bottom; my hair was blown out and I accentuated my makeup with red lipstick, while the sparkly diamond-embedded Louboutin's glistened on my feet.

After running around all day, I finally made it early to the restaurant; I had to have time to place name cards around the table. The predetermined seating arrangement was mostly to ensure my mother was seated as far away as possible from the people I partied with, just in case one of them pulled out a bag of cocaine at the dinner table.

Cassie helped me choose the seats, then spread bottles of Vodka around the lengthy table, which was already set with cold appetizers, and decorated with lily centerpieces. The spread of bright colors pleased me, but the vodka shot glasses next to each plate provoked my impatience.

The six-hour rush-around prior, combined with a furious hangover, had me feeling exhausted before the party had even started, and now I was feeling anxious about all of the guests arriving. My phone was blowing up with calls and text messages asking about directions, parking and various other things, from food and liquor selection to plans for the after party. My head was spinning with anxiety.

"Shot?" I asked Cassie as I opened a bottle of Vodka...

"Sure!" she replied.

"Shit, I haven't even eaten yet!" I laughed. It was normal for me to forget to eat. I had scheduled such a frantic life for myself that meals often slipped through the cracks.

"You forgot to eat again?!" Cassie gasped. "You should probably eat something other than vodka for breakfast!"

"You're right!" I said as I swallowed the liquor and grabbed a small piece of bread to soften the taste. "Another one?"

"No, you're nuts!"

"But it's my birthday," I guilted.

"Exactly…let's not make it your funeral."

So I took the shot alone. By now, my antics weren't even about impressing people. I was just completely out of control.

Soon all of the guests arrived and the celebration began. We ate, drank more vodka shots and chased them with red wine. Eating wasn't really my priority; I was laughing and making rounds talking to everybody. Here and there I'd snack on small bites, but nothing substantial.

After having a whole bottle's worth of vodka shots that were chased by half a bottle of red wine, I sat on a chair and spread some butter onto a small slice of bread. Dan approached me inconspicuously.

"Hey, Julia, you wanna go have a line?" he offered. "I got a bag for your birthday!"

"For sure," I responded, slurring my words and completely disregarding the fact that my family was here, and that a cocaine and alcohol cocktail with no food was a terrible idea.

We went down a flight of stairs to the shared bathroom. I felt invincible as I stumbled around while Dan lined up the drugs.

Now having a misconstrued conception of reality, I wanted to drink more; I took four more vodka shots at the table before I went to find Cassie.

I swayed carefully but confidently down the next flight of stairs, my head getting lighter and my balance harder to find. The rail I gripped onto led outside to where the party's smokers congregated.

"You look fucked," Cassie whispered quietly, trying to avoid my mother hearing.

"I'm fine!" I lied as my head began to spin.

"Yeah, then why are you swaying?" she laughed, not surprised by my careless attitude.

"OK, I'm going to the bathroom. See you upstairs," I told Cassie as I flapped my drunken arm in an attempted wave, before heading back up the stairs. That is the last thing I remember.

Blacking out was nothing new to me. It happened often when I partied. I would ingest so much drugs and alcohol that it was almost inevitable, and I would need to be reminded of the night's events the following day.

I also always felt the highest degree of a drug's effects. If I was drinking, I would be the drunkest person in the room—dancing with my eyes closed, leaning on my friends to stand up and stumbling all over the place. Somehow, I could do this for hours on end to be crowned "the last person to pass out."

When I did cocaine, I would gain enormous amounts of confidence and energy, bouncing up and around the walls; however, this would quickly turn to rage. Dan and I would fight and argue aggressively. Our tempers were always a short fuse when we were on the drug.

While smoking weed, my mind would fly high. I'd giggle endlessly and get insane munchies, eating anything and everything I could find in the house.

The drugs and alcohol took my mind off my lack of fulfillment in life, and they suppressed all thoughts of getting back on track. It was a constant battle. As if I had two contradicting voices in my head that rambled every waking moment of the day:

What are you doing with your life? You're better than this.

143

No you're not, what have you achieved?

Are you really going to miss the party? People are going to think you're lame if you miss out.

If you don't go, people will get angry with you.

You can't afford it. You need to save.

Screw saving. Go out, get wasted! It's been a hard week.

What happened to your dream of being a writer? You love to write.

No one is going to read your shit. Stop wasting time and enjoy your life!

I lost complete control of my mind, and the thoughts were driving me crazy. While I always took the partying to the next level, I never knew when to stop. And on this night, my foolish decisions caught up with me.

WAKE UP CALL

I woke to the sound of my mother, Cassie and Lisa screaming my name. My eyes felt congested, everything was blurry and I felt wet all over my face, legs and dress. As I regained consciousness, I realized I was lying on the bathroom floor.

"Ma'am, do you know where you are?" I heard from a man to my right. I looked over to see he was a paramedic.

"What happened, why is the ambulance here?" I asked, dazed and confused.

144

"Ma'am, can you please tell me your name?" he repeated.

"Julia... I'm fine," I snapped. I was annoyed, but at the same time I was sure that this couldn't be good.

I looked over at my mother; everything seemed to move in slow motion. Her face was pale and I could feel her devastation from across the room. She had no words. I had sucked every last bit of energy out of her and she worried for my life.

If I survived that night, she feared it was only a matter of time. I remembered the many times she had begged me to stop the drinking and partying. My mother had always said to me, that the worst thing a parent could do is to bury her child. In that moment, I made her fear a near reality.

After a brief examination, the paramedic was satisfied and began to pack up his bag. "She's going to be fine. Someone just needs to take her home," he said.

"Phew, it wasn't that bad," I declared. The girls didn't look impressed with my statement.

I looked around the bathroom as Cassie and Lisa helped me stand up; it looked like, in Cassie's words, a murder scene. There was red vomit in the sink, just liquid as I hadn't eaten much food. The vomit was in and around the toilet and all over the floor, no one knew if I slipped and knocked myself out or if I had passed out first.

As I stood up I felt the pain of the bruises everywhere. I touched my head and felt a huge bleeding lump. It must have been from the fall.

145

Cassie made arrangements to get me home, while Dan went out to party. Without saying "bye" to anyone, I got into the back of a friend's car and slept the entire way home.

Still heavily intoxicated, I stumbled into the house. Cassie helped me get undressed, shower and put my gown in the wash. We sat down at the balcony table; I was still completely wasted.

"Let's go out!" I joked, as if any of this was funny.

"You're an idiot!" Cassie replied, obviously not in a laughing mood.

"So what happened?" I asked.

"No idea. You went to the bathroom, and when you hadn't come back in a while, Lisa went down to look for you. She found you on the bathroom floor and called the ambulance. Your mother was throwing water on you, trying to wake you up."

"Lisa's an idiot. Why did she call the ambulance?" The magnitude of how severe this situation could have been was still beyond me.

"She was worried," Cassie replied. "Lisa came back up and asked Dan what he had given you. She kept yelling that it wasn't cocaine. We've all seen you in that state a million times, but you never throw up and you've never ended up on the floor like that. It was laced for sure."

"Wait, my mom heard that I had coke?" I stopped her.

"No, I don't think so. I think she went downstairs by then," Cassie continued. "By the time I had walked into the bathroom, it looked like a murder scene. They were freaking out because we couldn't wake you up for like 10 minutes."

"Oh shit, so who saw me like that?" I asked, my main concern being how I looked rather than the fact that I could have died.

I took a bad fall but it could have been so much worse. I was lucky to not have hit my head hard enough on the side of the sink or on the floor to get a head injury. I could have overdosed from the cocktail of alcohol and drugs. I could have had alcohol poisoning or stopped my heart completely.

The severity of what I was doing didn't even cross my mind. I was more concerned with "who saw" it.

"No one else, but is that really all you're worried about?" she said.

"Yeah, obviously, are you angry or something?" I asked.

"No, I'm not angry but, Julia, when are you going to stop taking this shit too far?" Cassie asked in a serious tone—a tone she didn't share too often, which gave it incredible power.

"It's my birthday, Cass, a one-off. Don't worry, it's cool," I laughed.

"I'm serious, Julia, you do this every weekend, and you're wasted or high almost every night. Maybe not to this extent, but still, it's a very risky game you're playing," she said. "I'm not joking when I say I'm going to take you on the show *Intervention.*"

"Don't worry, it's not that bad. Most of the time I don't even get that drunk," I lied. But she didn't buy it. Cassie had been listening to all of my stories and partaking in these antics for several years now. She knew exactly who I was.

Whether out loud or in my head, I couldn't admit my carelessness. My pride and ego was much too large. It wasn't until the next morning that I began to contemplate Cassie's warning.

Upon waking up, I was smacked with an excruciating hangover. And to make matters worse, I felt humiliated, lost and stupid. My reckless behavior made me sick.

I couldn't escape the only two questions circling in my head: *"What are you doing with your life?"* and *"Is this the woman you wanted to be?"*

I wanted so badly to be rid of last night's memories. So right then and there, I decided firmly that that would be the last time I did anything stupid like that again. But exactly one month later, it was Dan's birthday.

VERY BAD DECISIONS. PART 2.

"Hey! Is there room in your ride for me?" I asked, hoping to hitch a ride into the city for Dan's birthday celebration at club Boombox. Tessa (Dan's friend) usually drove into the city, meaning there would be a spare seat in the car.

"There's already five of us," Dan replied.

"OK, no problem, I'll see you down there," I said. I was annoyed Dan hadn't accounted for me to ride with them, but it was his birthday and I didn't want to make a fuss.

By the time I arrived at Boombox, it was already very late in the night and everyone was fairly drunk. I promised myself that Dan and I wouldn't have any drama tonight. Every time we went out these days, we had explosive arguments that led to screaming in the streets and smashing phones. I hated arguing in public. I would be so embarrassed as strangers walked by, but this happened every night out because of our heavy drinking and drug use.

Boombox was closing in three hours. And in my mind, this was a deadline. I had to drink as much as possible, to make the most of my night of course.

After the bar had closed, we made our way over to an after party, located in an apartment at the Casino. There, Dan handed me the powder I had been craving. Even though I had a desire to stop, I didn't think twice about accepting it.

My mental dependence on the drug was far greater than my desire for well-being or a better life.

We heard a fight break out between Tessa and her boyfriend, Kevin, and came running out onto the balcony. I only caught the end of it, seeing her flying across the floor from his push. Shocked, I ran over to help her up.

Bursting into tears, Tessa ran for the bathroom. I sat beside her on the icy tiles next to a toilet while she wailed tears of agony. I was repulsively too acquainted with these emotions, and I did my best to calm her down. Dan tried to settle Kevin, but he couldn't. Kevin left in a rage and we heard the door slam behind him.

Dan came to the bathroom where we were still sitting, and bleached our mood with more drugs.

"Tessa, Kevin took your car home," Dan said. "Let's go home, too?"

We decided to leave, so I convinced myself that I was sober and decided to drive. Tessa, Dan and I stupidly got in the car.

"Bump?" Dan offered a small peak of cocaine scooped on the end of a key. Without concern of my action's potential consequences, I leaned over and took it.

I turned on the car, blared the music and drove around the block to head home. Our biggest concern was getting caught, however, we assumed the chances of getting pulled over at 8 a.m. were slim.

Less than a minute into the journey, I drove around a corner toward the highway and saw the dreaded stop sign held by an officer. It was a random breath test: the only risk we had considered, and our most feared scenario.

"Shit!" Dan exclaimed. "OK, hold your breath when you count into the tube."

"No," Tessa interrupted, "just do it properly, act normal."

"Trust me," Dan said. "You can do this. I've seen people dodge the test before. We just gotta hope it's a counting device."

"They're going to know!" Tessa stressed.

Paranoia suffused the car, fear sent a spinning sensation through my head and waves of nausea hit my stomach. These were the most disgusting emotions I had ever felt.

"Everyone please stop," I yelled. "I can't fake the breath test. I'm going to try my luck, I should be fine."

"You got this, Jules," Dan comforted as I pulled up to the breath testing lane.

"Hello ma'am, you have been pulled over for the purpose of a random breath test," the officer said in a polite and friendly fresh morning tone. "Have you had any alcohol to drink during the night?"

"Just a couple, but it was hours ago so I should be fine," I stated.

"Great, I'll just get you to blow one long continuous breath into this device until I say stop," he continued, holding the decider of my destiny in his palm.

I blew into the device until I was instructed to stop, and then we awaited the reading.

"It's going to be fine," I continuously repeated in my mind, hoping for a reading below the 0.05 limit so we could go home. *"I haven't drunk that much, please don't do a drug test."*

"Miss, unfortunately, at this stage you're under arrest for the purpose of breath analysis," the officer announced. "The reading indicates you are above the legal limit. Please step out of the vehicle. You will need to come back to the station for a second breath analysis."

My heart dropped as my horror became my reality. I opened the door and stepped out of the car; each footstep in the elegant heels contrasted my new fate.

"We will wait here until you call!" Dan yelled out from my car as I lowered myself into the backseat of the police vehicle. The cage between the front and back seats amplified who I had become, and I was disgusted with myself.

What was I thinking? How am I going to tell my boss? I'm going to lose my job. What am I going to say to my mother? My thoughts were unbearable. I wanted more than anything to make my mother proud, but my actions continued to do the opposite. This would devastate her, again.

Suddenly, a distant memory flashed into my mind. I was a teenager, just busted for shoplifting. And I could hear the words of the officer who brought me home.

"I'm not planning on becoming a criminal!" my voice promised again.

"That's the thing, most of them don't plan on it either. Don't make us come see you again." the officer's voice echoed.

This is what he warned me about. My bad decisions were like a waterslide; I didn't plan to be here.

I was still high from the cocaine. Anxiety flooded my system, my breathing raced and adrenaline pumped through my blood. Each breath was short and unfulfilling; I desperately searched for any air of hope.

"How much was the reading?" I asked the officer as nicely and soberly as I could.

"Unfortunately, I cannot tell you until your second test is completed," he replied.

"Please, I am feeling a lot of anxiety. Can you tell me what are the possible outcomes here?" I cried, worried I would spend the night in jail.

"It depends on the reading, but hopefully you will blow under the limit and be free to head home," he said, slightly putting me at ease that I wasn't too far over.

The five-minute drive felt like hours. As we drove through an underground entrance into the car park, I observed a side of the police station I had never wished to see.

The officer unlocked the car, I stepped out and we proceeded towards the door, which he opened for me, as if I still deserved to be treated like a lady.

As I walked inside the back of the police station, I noticed the dark green double-stacked cells that lined the walls. The occupants' screams echoed through the frightful room, each yell tightening my muscles. The aggressive swearing and profanities pronounced this was not a joke.

"That's going to be me," I thought, knowing I wouldn't make it a night in this place.

The officer led me to a private, well-lit room; its white illumination emphasized my humiliation. I had become a disgrace and I felt complete fear of the unknown.

The interrogation intensified my nerves, as did the sound of chattering computer keys that documented my choices. The officer wasn't rushed, or maybe my distorted perception just made it seem that way. Nonetheless, the moment of truth was here.

"Please blow one continuous long breath into this device until I tell you to stop," he ordered as his words edged me closer to my fate. My palms sweated. And I gripped tightly on my knees in preparation. I took the tube into one hand, brought the mouthpiece to my lips and blew. I had now accepted that I deserved whatever was coming.

"How long will it take?" I asked nervously.

"A couple of minutes," he replied.

I couldn't take my eyes off the gray screen. It read "calculating breath analysis" for what seemed like forever. Then the result appeared: 0.049. I exhaled a breath of liberation; I was 0.001 under the legal limit. A narrow escape.

The officer drove me back to my car.

"That was very lucky," he said as we drove off.

"I know, but I didn't have much to drink so I was surprised by the reading in the first place," I defended. Luckily they did not do a drug test.

"You should still be more careful," the officer continued. "It doesn't take very much for something really bad to happen. I see it every day in this job."

"That's true," I replied.

"Even one drink slows down your response time, and this could prove fatal," he said.

I hadn't ever thought of it like that before. I had only imagined and expected that it would be a smooth and safe drive home.

"You're right," I admitted.

"I know it's not my place, but you seem like a nice girl," the officer said. "You should probably reconsider those friends, too. Good friends don't get in the car with you when you're drinking."

"It wasn't their fault," I replied.

"That guy you were with, he was a passenger in the car with another driver we pulled over…I think it was last weekend." He was referring to Dan.

Dan never told me about that. I began considering the officer's advice.

"Except that driver did turn out to be drunk, nearly double the limit...stupid," the officer continued. I stayed silent.

Dan and Tessa were still in the car when I returned. I drove us back to the house where the others had already heard the news that I was arrested. I joked with everyone about my triumph. But my arrogance was a façade. Even then, I knew this was the lowest I had gone. I *was* disgusted with my choices, but I didn't want to show vulnerability.

Tessa pulled me aside.

"Why did you drive anyway?" she asked. "You know I always drive. Why didn't you just park here before we went to Boombox and come into the city with us in my car?"

"Wasn't there already five of you?" I replied, knowing I was about to discover that Dan had lied to me.

"No, it was the same as always...Kevin, Sam, Dan and I. There would have been exactly one more seat in the car for you, I thought you would have come with us!" she declared.

"Next time," I smiled, refusing to break the promise I made to myself about fighting with Dan. "Now, let's drink it off! That bullshit completely sobered me up!"

I fronted to my friends, but I knew deep inside me that this was it. I had to change. I was certain that this was my last chance from God, The Universe or whomever: my final warning. I could have lost my license, in which case I would have lost my job. I could have spent the night in jail. And worst of all, I could have killed us or someone else. Again, this wasn't even a consideration when I decided to get behind the wheel.

As I idiotically sat on the couch, I pretended it was all a joke. But I couldn't help but reflect on my careless behavior. I zoned out, staring into the bright white wall in front of me. I contemplated the people I called my friends: the ones who got in the car with me and lined up drugs before we took off. Regardless of whether we got caught or not, our actions were so dangerous, and the potentially dreadful consequences didn't occur to any of us. Were we really that stupid?

I continued to drown my anxieties with more liquor. It was the only way I knew how to deal with my screaming conscience, telling me I had to change.

When I was sober, I hated my life and my choices. But I couldn't stop myself from making a bad decision. Everything I did revolved around drinking and drugs. The temptations were endless and the excuses were easy to find.

The world that I was comfortable in had a powerful way of keeping me stationary, and the people around me unintentionally encouraged my self-destruction. We were all so lost and confused. My conflicting thoughts made me desperately seek any escape.

FLOOR ME TWICE, SHAME ON ME

The night had now become a freezing winter morning, at 11 a.m. Tessa had gone to sleep in one room, while Dan, Kevin and I continued drinking. The other bedroom door was locked and Dan had the keys in his pocket.

"Dan, I'm cold, can you unlock the door to the room so I can grab a jumper?" I asked politely, trying not to disrupt their incoherent conversation.

"Yeah, give me a second," he replied dismissively.

I patiently waited, shivering in the cold for another 10 minutes. Assuming he had forgotten, I repeated the question. He brushed me off again. I waited a few minutes longer. Then, finally asked a third time...

"Hey, Dan, just pass the keys. I'm really cold," I said, trying not to nag. The cold was becoming unbearable.

"Man, I heard you!" he snapped. "Just fucking wait I said!"

Shocked, I looked over at Kevin through my blurry vision; he turned away to avoid my eyes. I looked back at Dan, "What is wrong with you?"

"Fuck's wrong with me? What the fuck's wrong with you?" he yelled as he stood up violently.

"Just let me get a jacket. Why are you being such a dick?" I yelled back.

"You're calling me a fucking dick. Fuck off bitch. Get out of here!" he responded.

"Fuck you, I will. Open the door so I can get my shit!"

He moved toward the hallway, blocking my only exit.

"Why are you standing there? How the fuck do you want me to leave if you're blocking the way? Open the fucking door!" I yelled. The cocktail of drugs and alcohol had now consumed both of our minds.

"Jump out the fucking window!" he commanded. "That's how you can fucking get out!"

I was sickened by his vicious words; he had completely lost his mind.

"Move out of the way!" I demanded as I stepped forward to get past him.

"No! Fucking jump out the window!" he yelled again irrationally. "I told you that's how you'll be getting outta here!"

I took the final step toward him. My right foot landed in position directly next to his.

Suddenly, the touch of both of his strong arms were on my shoulders, except it wasn't the same as it had ever been before. Without warning, I felt my feet fly out from under me. I no longer stood on the ground, and flew backwards across the floor.

With minimal effort, Dan had pushed me in the spur of the moment.

Lying on the cold floor, I noticed my high heels first. Why was I still wearing them? They made me so fragile and powerless. Then I came back to reality; my heels had nothing to do with my situation. I couldn't fight Dan.

My jaw dropped and my eyes widened as I looked into Dan's. His rage turned to remorse as he registered what had just happened. I used both hands to push myself up off the ground, and I then looked at Kevin still sitting on the couch. He saw me catch his eye this time. Then he stood up as if nothing had happened and walked into the other room where Tessa lay. Dan had such a power over his friends that they couldn't muster the courage to challenge him.

My next thoughts were awful: "*Maybe I am in the wrong, maybe I deserved it, or maybe it is just acceptable or normal now when men get mad. After all, Kevin just did the same thing to Tessa only a few hours before.*"

Before I was able to even get halfway up off the ground, Dan grasped me in his arms tightly.

"I'm sorry, I'm so sorry, I'm sorry. I can't believe I just did that. I'm so sorry!" he repeated over and over.

"Stop, let go of me," I insisted. "Open the door to the room."

He helped me up and walked behind me to the room.

"Please, are you OK?" he asked. "Please, don't leave. Let's talk about this. I am so sorry."

I was silent. I changed my clothes but I was too paralytically intoxicated to make a decision, so I sat down on the couch and began to cry. I didn't have words, just tears and a heavy sob that felt like my heart was about to leap from my throat.

For two hours, Dan held me in his arms, restating his apologies while I tried to stop weeping. I was so defeated that I couldn't move, but I had nowhere else to go.

The fall didn't hurt physically, but it broke me inside. The thoughts came rushing back in, this time in a new form: "*Why did he do this? I thought he loved me. How could he do it? He always prided himself on not being violent. He watched his mother get beaten badly by her former lover and he despised men who put their hands on women. What did I do so wrong to deserve it? Had the drugs completely fucked up his brain? Will he hit me properly next time?*"

And the most important thought: *"This life is not for me."*

Dan turned me over to face him, and he kissed my salty lips as he wiped the tears from my cheeks. I retracted and looked him straight in those same dark brown, compassionate eyes that I had found happiness in for so many years. The eyes I saw now were different. They made it clear that *this* man was no longer the person I knew.

Instead, it was a stranger in his form: an unknown person overcome by so much hatred, anger, adversity and disappointment. Everything around him was disorientated. Excessive alcohol, drugs and partying had changed the lovable, kind and good hearted person I once knew. All his choices were now made by a distorted mind.

As I looked into his dilated pupils, I could see a reflection of myself; then I realized I was seeing myself, too. I possessed the exact same characteristics and had gone through the same things—this was who *we* had both become.

We never spoke of it again. There was no need to. Dan exited my life the next day; both of us knew this chapter was over. My memories of us would only show me the good days, and I cried many times more because I couldn't hate him.

Instead, I remembered the day we were at the cemetery...

"Anytime, kiddo, you know I'll always look out for you." The image kept replaying in my mind.

I remembered coming home from Terri's office and telling him all about it. I remembered how supportive he was. How he held my hand as I overcame the death of my dad, and how I felt when I believed that: *Dan would be in my life forever. No matter the challenge, we could always count on each other.*

My belief was proved wrong.

The certainty of my once-faith in him no longer mattered; it no longer held any weight. And in its place, a new belief system was forming.

Though I could only remember good memories of Dan, inside I knew that the person I once loved so deeply was gone. And coming to grips with this reality was ripping me apart. I rang Simon. He always knew what to do, and I was too ashamed to tell anyone else; they all warned me about Dan, and I wasn't ready to hear *"I told you so."*

"What's wrong, bro?" Simon answered the phone.

"I need to come over," I cried.

"Then I'll see you soon," he replied. "Calm down though. Please drive safe here."

As I pulled into the driveway, memories flooded my mind. This time, his house brought me images of our childhood: running around giggling, throwing the ball. I remembered the many years I had pulled up in this same driveway as a teenager, and all of the problems that the walls had listened to us solve. The celebrations that took place here, and the losses we felt. When I was younger playing here, I never imagined this is how it would all end up. I could have never predicted that *this* girl would be walking into *this* same house years later, to tell Simon the events that just took place.

"What happened?" Simon asked. "Is your mom okay?"

"Yes, she's fine," I sobbed. "Dan pushed me onto the ground last night during a fight."

"What?" Simon replied. "Are you fucking kidding me? After everything you've done for that jerk... tell me what happened from start to finish!"

I told him the whole story without missing a detail. He looked at me in disgust.

"Bro, I don't give a fuck. No matter what happens, you don't put your hands on a woman," he began. "But listen, seriously, don't worry. At least you're not hurt. Well, you are... but not physically... you know, you're still in one piece. I will say, however, that if you ever think about going back when things are all fucking dandy again, I will personally slap the shit out of you...metaphorically speaking...too soon?"

I laughed as Simon went on.

"But all jokes aside, remember exactly how you feel right now in this moment. This needs to be the last of it."

I already knew that it was.

After countless let downs and pointless drama—fights, arguments, lies, drug and alcohol-fueled violence, comedowns, hangovers and tears—I landed on the floor... I guess it's true when they say: *sometimes you just need a really good fall to see where you stand.*

I decided that I had had enough. Somewhere deep down I knew I wanted to write, speak and help people. I knew that my actions were in no way reflecting that or getting me there, and I believed intensely that there had to be a better life.

Regardless of how hard it would be, I knew there had to be something better. This soul consuming world was eating me alive.

The other side simply had to be brighter, so I began to move towards it. The coming months felt like I was walking in the dark, but they were necessary. For what was next to come would be a new chapter in my life, a positive turn for this book.

These dark days were the birth of a true inspiration that was always inside of me, begging to be released.

Lessons

BECOME THE PERSON YOU ARE MEANT TO BE

To create fulfilment in the Social area of life, there is one specific place you must start. You may not like it, but I will unapologetically say: it's time to forgive.

Forgive the best friend for the way she acted. Forgive the guy who hurt you. Forgive the partner that broke your trust. And forgive the people who let you down.

Forgiveness is necessary. And not forgiving only hurts you and holds you back. I am sorry you feel that you have been hurt, my dear friend reading, but release yourself from this pain, because you are the only one feeling it. Don't let other people's actions or behavior change who you are.

Know that to the person who hurt you, it isn't about you. Everybody is just trying to find their own happiness; everybody wants to be loved and appreciated.

Once we can stop labeling everything as either good or bad, the whole concept of forgiveness becomes redundant. Every scenario can be interpreted either way, depending on your perspective. So be lenient on people's mistakes, and forgive them fast. People are simply just doing the best they can, with what they know. We are all in search of all the same things: to belong, be happy and safe, and everyone is fighting a battle that nobody knows about.

One of my favorite pieces ever written was from a novel called *Shantaram* by Gregory David Roberts:

"Sooner or later, fate puts us together with all the people, one by one, who show us what we could, and shouldn't, let ourselves become. Sooner or later we meet the drunkard, the waster, the betrayer, the ruthless mind, and the hate-filled heart. But fate loads the dice, of course, because we usually find ourselves loving or pitying almost all of those people. And it's impossible to despise someone you honestly pity, and to shun someone you truly love."

Recently a friend of mine said to me, "Julia, you can't just be so trusting of everybody, that girl completely took advantage of you!"

"Why?" I responded. "Yes, that girl took advantage of me, and it was hurtful, but there were probably 20 other people who helped me, appreciated me, encouraged and loved me for who I am. I think I'll keep being 'me' and take those odds."

Remember also, that we co-create our circumstances, and accept that you have played an equal role in their creation, too. Be yourself. And focus on how doing so brings out the good in people and the good in you. Learn from each person and respond accordingly, but never change your values because you got burned.

Contrast is not bad. It makes you explore and discover what you want and what you don't want. Often we need an intense enough situation to create a sincere desire that propels us to walk away, or overcome any obstacle in life.

I didn't want to leave Dan and my comfort zone world behind; I was scared to death. More than anything, I wanted to help and take him with me into a better life. He wasn't ready to go, I had to. I had no other choice but to unlink the last piece of cargo that was weighing me down.

The truth is, the people around you are a reflection of you. How you act is who you attract.

Self-destructive behavior was my way to feel balanced and reset. Ironically it was doing the exact opposite. When I went out and partied in the clubs every weekend, I felt cool, wanted and a part of something. I felt that the people I hung out with loved and cared about me, but this proved not to be the case. What I was putting out was what I was getting, and these habits made no room for anyone else.

HOW TO ATTRACT GOOD PEOPLE INTO YOUR LIFE

Attracting happy, inspired and ambitious people is not difficult. All I had to do was spend my time somewhere else, and become like the people I wanted to meet.

The result I wanted, the life I wanted, was not aligned with my actions. The wasted days, depression and a very unstable mind were the results of my erratic, destructive behavior.

Everything I was doing was in my comfort zone. Therefore, not many people could see the cracks in my smoke and mirrors. The worst part was that I had actually convinced myself that this was "fun" and that this was simply who I was.

Alone, I usually felt unhappy. People often said, "You need time to think." But when I had time to think, this made room for my negative thoughts. I hated being questioned, I hated conflicting opinions and I didn't want to separate from the lifestyle (and things) that I had created, even if it was fake and unfulfilling, because "at least we got it on the #gram."

So how do we make it so that we are surrounded by uplifting, positive people and have meaningful friendships?

We start by being nice and being friendly always—yes, always. I know, not exactly rocket science, yet it is still not happening out there. You might be thinking *I am nice!* Which I am sure you are most of the time, almost always! But I'm also talking about when you have a bad day at work, when you're stressed out, when someone dies or you go through a breakup. I'm talking about being nice to any person you come in contact with: a stranger, customer, boss, employee or homeless person. Never excuse yourself from being nice. Take full control of your emotions, regardless of what is going on around you.

Find something to like in every person and find something you can relate to. I promise, there is always something you can relate to if you try. Remember, we all have the same qualities in different quantities. Make a conscious effort to like people, I mean everyone, even if they don't like you.

Make people feel good and do something unnecessary; nothing lifts a person like being respected and valued. Regularly tell your family and friends that you love them. You never know when you will miss your chance. And point out people's positive aspects more often than giving constructive feedback.

Be what I call a "Life-Brightener": figure out your most likeable qualities and share them with everyone you meet. If you're unsure of what they are, ask your closest friends or family members what they like about you. Once you've identified these qualities, share them with the world and spread more of that magic everywhere!

Be where you are with *who* you are there with. Put away your phone. Or if it's important, then excuse yourself and wrap up your conversation quickly (many of us could do more of this one, including me sometimes!). But like it or not, people don't like to waste their time with others whose minds are somewhere else on the phone.

Do what you can to improve other people's lives and always wish them good things; there is plenty of room for us all to win. Remember, successful people are not selfish, and being wealthy only amplifies the personality you already have.

Landing on the ground made me realize I wanted more from life and that my current actions and behavior were not only extremely unfulfilling, but also depressing. They drained all my energy and scattered my mind. And worst of all, I had no purpose.

To attract good people into your life, you need to portray your ideal qualities first—you need to be the type of person you wish to attract. Otherwise, these people simply won't want to be around you. Call it the "law of attraction," "the law of giving and receiving" or whatever you'd like, the fact is, they won't spend a moment with you if your behavior, actions and mindset are not on their wavelength.

The Social area of life made a huge impact on my journey to Best Life-ing. But only after I made the choice to change and let go of my anger. The people you spend most of your time with are a reflection of you, your internal thoughts and feelings.

When you surround yourself with kind and honorable people, intelligent and inspired people, you will become better just from their presence.

WHO IS IN YOUR TOP 5?

You may have previously heard that *"you are the average of the five people you spend your time with,"* but did you know that you also *earn* the average of the people that you spend your time with?

It makes sense to think that the conversations we choose would vary for people with different jobs and incomes. For example, a group of hedge fund company owners or investors are going to have different discussions in their spare time in comparison to a group of authors. What you talk and think about the most is what shapes your reality.

Don't worry, I am not saying to get rid of all of your friends who don't make you better or earn a certain amount of money; I'm saying spend *more* of your time with the people you aspire to be like. These are simply the people you want in your top five.

Examine how the people you spend your time with make you feel. Energized or drained, challenged or stagnant, positive or negative, happy or sad. Notice what the conversations are about—other people, personal goals, dreams or aspirations?

Choose your top five wisely and spend time with number six only when you can.

And if there are toxic people in your top five, reevaluate if there is a need to spend time with them at all. Remember, no one can control your actions but you. So don't blame or judge toxic people for your behavior.

This goes back to my McDonald's customer story from earlier. Remember the guy who was mad about missing his BBQ sauce? Would he be so angry if he wasn't so consumed by his judgement and expectations of others? If it wasn't for his own anger, would he have a need to behave in such an aggressive way towards others?

We can get so consumed in our own self judgements that we project this onto other (usually undeserving) people. And oftentimes, the judgements we make are pointless. Once we stop judging pointless things about other people, we stop judging pointless aspects of ourselves, too. This gives us more confidence, patience and understanding. Why do we want these admirable qualities? They enable you to accept and push past adversity to truly live your best life.

If you are open to receiving others' gifts, every person you meet will add some sort of value to your life. What they look like, their physical features, the clothes they wear, their hairstyle and how tall they are does not matter. Worry more about how people make you feel. You never know who you might connect with.

Simultaneously, forget having power over others. We cannot control other people, and it is not our job, nor is it our privilege. Let others live their life however they please, and focus your energy into living *your* life in the way that pleases you.

Don't pretend to be happy if you are not. If one of your top five's way of life doesn't work for you, then (without drama) tell him or her and allow their decision to adapt or to not adapt to what you seek. Allow the other person to do the same and candidly share their feelings about you. Worst case, (if done properly) you can still maintain a healthy relationship and do things that are in line with both of your values.

It is important to know that if you want to spend time with someone, you need to do things that are high on *their values,* things that are important to *him or her.* But, be sure not to confuse this with doing things that you don't want to—it will be hard to find fulfilment in that, and it will mess up your fulfilment in the other areas of life.

If you're ever unsure about a task, always measure it based off how you feel after doing it, not before. For example, how do you feel *after* going to the gym? How do you feel *after* drinking excessively and partying all night? How do you feel *after* spending time with a particular friend? If it is not aligned with what you want, stop wasting your precious time on it (trust me on this one).

Figure out what is good for you and find people who want to do it with you, or do it alone and meet people whose interests already align with yours.

In order to be able to do, have or feel anything worthwhile, you must love and respect yourself first and make room for what you want. One, because you cannot truly give love and respect to other people if you can't give it to the most important person in your life first—you. And two, think about it…you cannot party every night *and* start your dream business, because your time, energy and money is invested in one or the other. You have to *choose* which one you want to sacrifice for the other because you already *are* always sacrificing anyway; it's just a matter of *what.*

If you are stuck and unfulfilled in the Social area of life, believe that there is a better life out there. There are so many incredible people in this world with breathtaking stories, extraordinary achievements and passionate dreams. Sometimes you will have to walk away from relationships and open your mind, sometimes without having any idea of where you're going. Even if there may only be a *hope* that life will get better, start walking anyway. It is a very fruitful road.

CHOOSE TO SEE THE GOOD IN PEOPLE AND PAST EXPERIENCES

At the end of the day, every person makes a positive impact on your life, if you choose to view it in that perspective. Even the people who seem like villains in my stories, have helped pave the way to my new, best life. All of *these* people made an enormous, positive impact on my life, not only on the good days but also in the moments I perceived to be bad at the time. Some showed me what I wanted in life, and others showed me what I didn't want my life to become. Others helped force me out of situations I no longer wanted but had previously created.

I know I have taken you on a journey through my story, where I have painted a picture of characters who you may now see as heroes or villains. I did this deliberately to show you how I felt about them in each moment as it was lived.

Now I want to show you that perspectives can change, and I'd like to ask you to let go of any beliefs you may have about the so-called villains that I had created and the ones you might create in real life. I would like to take you on a journey with me. We are going to use a couple of examples to forgive them and understand how they may have possibly felt during those moments.

If you are or know a person like Dan, we know he is a good person with good intentions. Life experiences have taught him how to respond, and not every response in life will be perfect or even correct for that matter. We know Dan is also trying to find his way and his own version of happiness. We know Dan never means harm, and we know that everything happened the way it was meant to, to lead to the next chapter of life for everyone involved—we all greatly benefited from this blessing in disguise. We wish nothing short of love, and believe he will find his passion, peace and joy.

If you are or know a person like Lisa, we thank you for looking out for your friends. We know your intentions are good and pure. We know you are able to find the strength to overcome any beliefs that limit you. We wish only wonderful blessings in your life and the feeling of fulfilment in all areas. We hope you will dream and make your reality everything you can imagine and much more.

Forgiveness is not about them, their actions or what we may perceive them to have done wrong. It is about you and freeing yourself from any anger that you feel towards others who may have hurt you. It's about releasing yourself of self-pity and taking control of your own emotions and, in turn, your life. Live only love towards everybody, regardless of how they may feel about you.

Diary Entry

January 13th, 2018 – Sydney, Australia

THE DREAMS, THE FRIENDS, THE ACTIONS OR SIMPLE MATH: DREAMS + SOCIAL CIRCLE = ACTION

"Bernard, there's something I want to talk to you about," I began.

"What is it?" Bernard replied.

"You know how I've always wanted to move to Miami?"

"I do."

"I think it's time," I said.

"OK, tell me what your plan is."

"Well, I don't exactly have a solid plan, but I can't find any reason that is holding me back," I said. "I am out of debt and have savings now, I am single and have no kids, I'm not afraid anymore and I believe I can make it no matter what. Plus, worst case scenario, the move doesn't work out and I'll come back. At least I will have tried. You know, it's been a long-time dream of mine and it feels like it's now or never. There's nothing holding me back!"

"And why do you want to move to Miami so much?" Bernard asked.

"I've been traveling there for 10 years now…you know for work and holidays… and I've just fallen in love with the place. The warm sunny weather, the unlimited opportunity, the blue skies and green trees, the warm beach…" I explained. "But most of all, it's the people. I have completely fallen in love with them. My group of friends in Miami are some of the most incredible, inspiring and kind hearted people that I have ever met."

"I see," Bernard replied.

"Aside from you of course," I laughed. "But seriously, I need to spend at least a portion of my life out there. I want these friends to be a part of my life; they make me the happiest I've ever felt."

"I agree. Do you think you're ready?" Bernard asked.

"I do, besides, I think I've done everything I needed to here in Sydney. It's time to get out of my comfort zone, challenge myself to the limit and finish writing my book."

"If you think you're ready, I believe you can do it!"

"Holy moly… I'm moving to Miami!" I announced.

A year later, my good friend (and roommate) sat in my Miami bedroom every night for a week as I read aloud to him the pages of this book.

KEY POINTS:

1. Determine what you value and make decisions based on how you feel after doing something.

2. You are the average, and you earn the average, of the top five people you spend your time with.

3. Stop judging people, and you will stop judging yourself.

4. To attract like-minded people, you must be a pleasant person to be around.

5. Free yourself by forgiving others. The people who cross your path are necessary for your experience, and every situation is co-created.

ACTION STEPS:

1. Identify judgemental thoughts; we all have them at some point, so practice noticing and then releasing them.

2. When spending time with people, analyze whether they make you feel good or drain you. Don't evaluate their behaviors or actions, only assess your feelings when you're around them. Based on those feelings, allocate the time you spend with them accordingly.

3. Write down the top five things you deeply want in your life. Look at the top five people you spend your time with. What do you do, and discuss in this time? Does it align with what you want?

Chapter Seven

MOMENTUM

AREA OF LIFE 6/7: PHYSICAL

It was mid April of 2016. After leaving my old world behind, I had been walking in what felt like the dark for five months now. I had just hit my rock bottom moment with Bernard.

Life had changed, but it didn't feel better. And this lonely walk came with no promises that it would end.

The day following my breakdown to Bernard, I woke up a little earlier with a little bit of motivation. My first mission was to lose weight.

Having never really exercised before, I planned to start with 30 minute walks; so I put on my running shoes, plugged in my ear-phones and began my new morning fitness routine.

That motivation lasted about three days.

Being extremely unfit, I found even the smallest of tasks tremendously difficult. But I had to push on. So I tried to shift my mind away from the negative thoughts; I listened to audio books and looked for small ways to appreciate any beauty I found.

AN OLD FRIEND FROM MY PAST REAPPEARS

I met Anthea back when I first started at McDonald's as a kid. For the first time in a few years, she and I caught up, after my walk.

"How's everything going?" Anthea said.

"It's been good, I haven't seen you in ages. You live just up the road. How come you never visit?" I asked.

"Do you want me to be honest? Don't hate me," she said hesitantly.

"Yes I want you to be honest and, of course, I won't hate you!" I confirmed.

"I didn't like Dan. I knew he was bad for you and you didn't listen; it just irritated me every time I came here, knowing that he was using you and destroying your life."

"He wasn't destroying it, I was doing that myself. But that's no excuse, Anthea, we could have met at the sports club or something?"

"And would you not have told me the stories of what he had done that week?" she replied.

I pondered her question. I knew she was right. I was the toxic person in her experience and she was simply keeping me out of her top five.

"I know we could have met somewhere, but I gave you a lot of advice and you just didn't listen," Anthea continued. "It felt like every time we met up you just wanted to complain about it, and to be honest that's a waste of my time."

Her words were harsh, but truthful, confirming the advice I shared in the previous chapters—be enjoyable to be around and, remember, successful people want to know that you value their time.

"I understand that. I didn't see it back then, but I appreciate you being honest with me," I said, without getting upset or defensive. This was my chance to listen and get better, and I was grateful for her feedback.

"OK, so on a more positive note," Anthea changed the subject, "I heard from Bernard that you are working on yourself and trying to lose weight. How is this going?"

"Good, I've just started to go for walks regularly and read more."

"I told you, once you get older you're going to have to do something to keep off the weight," she laughed. "You should join the gym with me, I'm looking for a new one right now."

"No way, I prefer to just hang out in nature and enjoy the fresh air," I replied.

"Just trust me, you might like it. Give it a go!" Anthea encouraged.

"Nah, I cant really afford it anyway. I'm trying to get out of debt."

"OK, well if you change your mind, let me know."

After Anthea left, I scrolled through Facebook and saw an ad that read: *new personal training program for women! 4-week challenge, only $20/week.* I took a screenshot of the ad and sent it to Anthea.

"OK, I found this cheap one. Let's give it a shot," I messaged. "How strange that I came across this right after we talked about it!"

BEST *Life-ing*

It wasn't really strange though. All of our opportunities come from where we focus our attention.

"Yes, I'm in!" Anthea responded. "Let's start tomorrow."

THE DREADED FIRST GYM CLASS

Walking into my first gym session, I remembered my first day at the new school where I had met Simon.

My fears of not fitting in came rushing back. I wanted to leave. Self-conscious thoughts polluted my mind: "*I'm not fit enough to go to the gym, I don't know how to use the machines, everyone will laugh at me, I'm the fattest person here.*"

"Anthea," I said, "this is a bad idea. I'm going to just go for a walk in the park."

"Julia, stop!" she commanded, grabbing my right arm as I turned to walk away. "You're going to be fine. I was nervous the first time I trained, too. Come on, if you don't like it, we just won't come back."

I held my breath as I signed the waiver, then followed Anthea into the class training room.

The sun beaming through the large industrial windows emphasized my insecurities. I squirmed. I felt like I was standing on a stage with a hot spotlight pointing directly at me. As the crowd gathered, I knew my performance was approaching fast and they were all going to see me, except I hadn't rehearsed for this show.

"Alright!" the trainer whooped, breaking my metaphorical thoughts with his loud entrance. "Welcome to the class! We have a few new friends joining us. Let's give a huge, warm welcome to Anthea and Julia."

"Great, now the whole room is going to stare at us," I thought as their roaring applause exacerbated my stomach's already panicked butterflies.

"Anthea, I want to leave," I whispered.

"Let's begin!" the trainer yelled.

"Too late," Anthea whispered back.

I couldn't decide what would be more embarrassing: to run out of the room, or display my shockingly awkward version of a push up. I tried to ignore those thoughts. Doing my best to follow along and keep up, I began to feel dizzy and nauseous.

"OK, great work everyone!" the trainer praised. "Now that the warm up is done, let's get straight into it."

"What? That was just the warm up?" I whispered to Anthea. "I'm going to die!"

"Haha, you'll be fine," she laughed. "Just do what you can."

Every moment was a struggle to get through; I was pushing myself harder than ever before. I was completely out of breath and parts of my body that I didn't know existed were in raging pain. My legs and arms shook just trying to get through it. I wondered how the other students were managing.

I glanced around the room and quickly noticed that everyone found this class difficult, even the experienced people who perfectly mastered every

181

posture; it was just difficulty at *their* own level. Nobody was looking at me, that was until I caught eyes with an older lady; she gave me a big bright smile and a thumbs up, which let me know that it was going to be okay. I was going to get through this and nobody was judging me.

"OK, now our finisher will be to plank for 60 seconds," the trainer announced. This meant that the 45 minutes had come to an end. I had made it!

"Come on guys, you can do anything for 60 seconds," the trainer encouraged us.

"That's true," I thought. *"I can do anything for 60 seconds."*

As the class came to an end, I followed Anthea's lead to pack up the mats and dumbbells. A lady walked towards me, the same one who smiled at me in class. She paused and placed her hand softly on my shoulder.

"How did you find it? Your first time in the class?" she asked.

"It was OK, I'm just happy I got through it," I replied, wiping the sweat from my forehead.

"What are you complaining about? I'm 64 years old," she laughed. "You girls did great. Don't worry, it gets easier…sort of!"

Anthea and I laughed as the lady picked up her bags and walked away. She left us with a feeling of assurance that it was all going to be okay. I began to feel a sense of positivity about the whole experience.

"How was it, girls?" The trainer approached us.

"It was great!" Anthea replied, being sure to not give me a chance to respond negatively.

"Awesome! You girls smashed it! So I'll see you again at Wednesday's class," he said enthusiastically.

"Absolutely!" she spoke for both of us as she nudged my arm.

As we walked to the car I was still trying to catch my breath.

"See that wasn't so bad!" Anthea said excitedly.

"It was actually OK and, surprisingly, everyone was really nice," I replied.

"I knew you'd love it! Great, now we can be gym buddies!"

"Anthea, 'love' is a strong word, and 'gym buddies' might be too soon. I want to take this relationship slow," I laughed. "But seriously, that trainer was really good. The way he ran that class, he reminded me of a motivational speaker."

"I was thinking the same thing!" Anthea replied. "He really was like a motivational speaker."

Funnily enough, turns out he was.

"Yeah, I've been reading this book called *The Law of Attraction*, so many things he said in the class sounded similar."

"Finally, you've started reading that book!" Anthea laughed. "You've had it for years."

"I know," I agreed. "I've actually read a few books this month. I'm learning a lot."

HEALTHY HABITS GIVE BIRTH TO A NEW BUSINESS

My new daily routines started to create good habits. Instead of drinking and partying all the time, I now read books and took time out for silence and meditation. I didn't recognize the magnitude that these small changes would soon make to my overall life, and the opportunities that would become available to me once I aligned my actions with my dreams.

The newfound hours in the week were now used to research healthy eating, read for an hour per day, practice 10 minutes of silence and meal prep on Sundays—using the new healthy recipes I had learned that week.

Within a few weeks I became obsessed with the gym. We attended multiple classes and enjoyed every moment of it. I wanted to live at the gym. The environment was so supportive and positive. We made new friends and I felt more vibrant and more alive from eating healthy and being active. I felt strong and I could see the progress that both Anthea and I were making, not only because we were losing weight, but our strength and endurance was growing.

I started to work one-on-one with a personal trainer, mainly because I didn't know how to use most of the equipment and further progress with my training outside of classes. Ron became my trainer. He was supportive and encouraging, and he helped grow my confidence and build on my health and fitness knowledge. Ron was always happy to answer any questions, and I fell even more in love with the gym.

"I know you said you just wanted to learn how to use the equipment, but what's your overall health goal?" Ron asked at the end of our first session.

"I don't really have one to be honest. It would be really cool if I could do a chin-up one day," I replied hesitantly.

"We'll get you there!" Ron laughed. "All the girls seem to want is to do a chin-up, haha."

"What about your food, do you cook at home or eat out more often?" Ron continued.

"I actually stopped eating out a few months ago. I'm trying to save money, but I have really fallen in love with cooking lately," I replied.

"That's good, what kind of food do you cook?" he asked.

"Well, I like to be a little bit 'extra.' I have been cooking gourmet restaurant style meals," I laughed.

"Have you got any pics?" Ron asked.

"Yeah, actually, I do," I replied as I reached for my phone to show him.

"Wow, these look incredible! Are you a chef?"

"No," I laughed. "I just Google an image of a fancy meal and try to recreate it in a healthy way."

"That's awesome! I'd love to try it one day!"

"Next time I cook, I'll bring you one!" I replied. "I better head off to work, I'm going to be late, but thanks for showing me everything. It was a great session."

I arrived at work, starving from the big workout we had just done. I walked up to the microwave and heated up a meal I had cooked yesterday: a delicious steak eye fillet with spicy blackberry and red wine jus, on ginger sweet potato mash with a side of green beans and broccolini.

The fragrance filled the room and caught my coworkers' attention.

"Wow! Where did you order that from? It looks and smells amazing," my colleague said as he approached.

"Haha, I made it myself," I laughed.

"I will pay you to cook like that for me, your food always looks delicious."

"I mean, I could if you want me to. I'm already cooking so it won't hurt to just double the recipe. Just throw in $50 for the grocery bill."

"Sounds good to me!" he exclaimed.

That night I went home and decided to plan and prepare a few meals that I would cook for my colleague and I. I also made an extra one for Ron as I had promised.

"Here's the meal I said I would make for you," I smiled as I handed Ron the box of goodness after our session.

"Wow, thank you. I didn't think you would actually do it," he replied in surprise. "This looks great, I can't wait to try it."

"You're welcome! Of course, I said that I would and I'm a woman of my word!" I laughed, waving bye as I ran out to head to work.

Later that afternoon, Ron wrote me a message: *Just tried your meal. It was absolutely amazing. Thank you so much for bringing it in for me, that was really kind of you. But seriously, you should do it for real. Me and many people I know would be keen to buy these meals.*

This started happening all around me. There seemed to be a pull toward this meal prepping thing. The following week, I dialed Anthea's number on my way home one night after work.

"Hey, I have an idea, but I'm going to need your help," I said.

"What is it?" Anthea asked.

"Well, a colleague from work asked me to cook for him. He loves my meals and now he wants me to cook for his mom, girlfriend and sister," I began.

"OK…" Anthea replied.

"Then, three other people at work heard about it and asked if I could cook for them, too, so I agreed," I continued. "Also, Ron at the gym tried one of my meals and he loved it, too. I'm thinking we should start a little meal prep business."

"That's actually a good idea," Anthea responded. "Everybody loves your food and we have been telling you to open your own restaurant! We've even already named it for you."

For years, my friends had been calling dinner at my house "Juu's Kitchen."

"I know, but this could be so much better. I get so excited every time someone tries my food," I said. "But seriously, I can't do this without you."

"OK, I'm coming over, let's work out the plan!"

We worked late into the night on our new hobby, and quickly our first day of meal prepping for others approached.

JUU'S KITCHEN OPENS FOR BUSINESS

On Sunday, May 28th, 2017, we received a total of 50 meal orders. At 7 p.m., I just arrived home from a six-hour getaway back to Sydney. Anthea met me at the grocery store, and we shopped for two hours before beginning to cook. The plan was to have everything finished by midnight.

At 2 a.m., we looked around the kitchen; it was a complete mess: half prepared meals, half chopped vegetables, pots of boiled sweet potato and rice, as well as raw meat still sitting in the fridge, unseasoned and still packaged. We looked at each other, both defeated.

"Holy shit, we still have so much to do. We are going to be here all night!" Anthea shrieked.

The realization of an imminent all-nighter sank in, but the worst was yet to come.

"At least we've got each other," I replied, hardly believing my own pitiable attempt to lift the mood.

But it was true, there is no way I could have done all of this by myself. So in that moment I realized how grateful I was to have my friend by my side, helping me with this challenging, yet exciting new project. Four hours later at six in the morning, we stood, depleted on the cold tiles of my Sydney apartment's kitchen. We finally finished preparing our first 50 meals. It was cause for celebration. But we were beat. And our complaining confirmed our exhaustion.

Every part of my body hurt, from the excruciating discomfort in my legs, to my burning feet and all the way through my throbbing arms and shoulders, to my pounding head. My brain felt like mush and I could hardly compose a sentence anymore.

Aside from this, we were anxious that something would go wrong. Maybe people wouldn't like the taste of our food, or maybe it would be too spicy for some. Were the portions big enough? And was everything cooked thoroughly yet not overcooked?

We packed the meals into green-checkered bags, labeled them and loaded up a grocery trolley that we found in the hallway outside the elevator. I drove the meals around until 11 a.m. When I arrived back home, my bed was paradise and I collapsed into one of the deepest sleeps imaginable.

Waking up the following morning presented us with more reason than ever to persevere. Messages, from all of the people I had delivered meals to, were lighting up my phone. They praised us about the taste, portion size and quality of the food. This made it all feel worth it.

"I want to cry tears of joy," Anthea said, thankful that our fears did not turn out to be the reality.

"Do you think we will pull this off again?" I replied with uncertainty.

"What do you mean pull it off again? We are going to do double next week!" Anthea asserted enthusiastically.

And double was exactly what we did. After getting through our first week and receiving positive feedback, I decided to share photos of our meals on social media.

I never expected the insane response we got. Over 100 meals were ordered for week two of Juu's Kitchen. Though this was great, there was no way we could pull this off in my small home kitchen. To systemize the meal prep process, I decided to use the business skills that I had learned in the job that I didn't appreciate. So the following day, I arranged for us an industrial kitchen.

The next problem was that neither Anthea nor I were professional chefs. In fact, we could hardly figure out how to turn on the stoves and oven. What's more, this number of meals ordered would take us way too long to cook. So we hired a chef who was willing to prepare my recipes for our second night of professional meal prepping.

The first night of cooking over 100 meals had fast approached. Due to the short notice, our Chef Brian had agreed to come work at Juu's Kitchen after finishing a 10-hour shift at his restaurant job. Anthea and I didn't like the idea, because we knew he would be tired, but Brian insisted he would be okay. He had done long shifts like this before; in our desperation and panic, we agreed.

At 7 a.m. after 10 hours of cooking overnight, Brian was clearly exhausted. There was still a lot to do, but we felt really bad for him and asked him to go home and get some rest.

"OK, thank you," Brian said. "I have the beef tenderloin still in the oven, it just needs four more minutes before it is done. I am exhausted!"

"Thank you so much, Brian. Have a good sleep," I replied.

As Brian left, the photographer that we had arranged walked in and began setting up for the website photoshoot.

"Hi Julia, I'm going to set up over here if that is OK," Rob the photographer said.

"Yes, that's perfect. I will be out with the first round of dishes soon," I smiled, although I was feeling panic, knowing we were quickly falling behind.

Anthea and I began plating in a hurry while still trying to maintain the attention to detail and presentation of each dish for the photos. Anthea would bring out each plate as I began to assemble the next; we were rushing, breaking things and running around like maniacs.

So much was happening at once. Time was flying past us faster than ever before, and in the midst of all the chaos, we were making big mistakes.

"Shit! We forgot the beef tenderloin in the oven!" I yelled as I ran for the oven door, gripping both scorching handles with my bare hands. "Ahhhhhhhh!"

"Are you okay?" Anthea ran over in a panic.

"Not even close," I replied, trying to decide what hurt more—my hands or the $700 worth of burnt steak we had no replacement for. To make matters worse, we were running out of time to fix it.

We rushed to the closest store to buy more meat at full price, and began to cook it all again. Finally, after 16 long hours, we had finished cooking and packing all of the food. The next four hours we had to drive it to our customers.

When I finally got home after this 20 hour day, I collapsed in my bed, thinking I never wanted to do this again. Yet again when I woke up, I felt like it was all worth it because of the grateful messages we received from our happy customers.

MOMENTUM LEADS TO NEW OPPORTUNITIES

I kept going, day by day. In the weeks and months that passed, Anthea helped me get the business set up. But she eventually couldn't do it anymore. Her life was changing and she and her husband were trying to have a baby. She no longer had the time to commit.

I wasn't ready to give it up. We had done so much work, had built up a reputation and grown a regular customer base that I didn't want to disappoint. All of my focus shifted to making my clients happy. I had developed such a passion for it that the hard work was easy to push through.

One Saturday morning on the way home from an 8 a.m. session, I stopped by the grocery store to grab some eggs for breakfast. I noticed Al, an old friend that I hadn't seen in over five years, standing in the aisle.

"Hey!" I called out. "How random, I haven't seen you in so long!"

"I know, it's been ages!" Al replied as he gave me a hug.

"What are you doing here in this area?"

"Just moved here recently," Al replied.

"Nice, do you still have the same number? We should catch up!"

"Yeah I do, sure, we can grab a drink tonight," Al offered.

"Great, I have a few things I need to get done today, and then I'll give you a call. You better answer the phone!" I laughed.

Al was notorious for switching off his phone and disappearing for months at a time. This would occur after Al joined my friends and I for a wild weekend bender. He'd party with us and then stop speaking with us, likely because of the mental, physical and financial toll of our high-octane, alcohol-fueled weekends. Despite my multiple attempts over the years, I could never get a hold of him, so I eventually gave up. In hindsight, Al was likely trying to keep us out of his top five. Regardless, I was excited to see him at the grocery store and really hoped that we would catch up. My instincts told me there was something I could do to help, even though I had no idea what was wrong.

That night we caught up at a local bar, and Al opened up to me for the first time in a very long time.

"What's up, man, where have you been all this time?" I asked.

"I've just been keeping it low. I'm tired of drinking and partying, and I don't really know where I'm headed in life," Al began.

"Trust me, I know the feeling well. I was there just a few months ago," I comforted. "But then everything began to change, and once I got the momentum going, it started to feel inspiring. Now I can't wait to get out of bed in the mornings. You'll do the same."

"I don't know, I'm not as tough as you," he said.

"Trust me, I'm not tough at all. Walking away from everything was the hardest thing I've ever done, but it also turned out to be the best thing I have ever done so far," I replied. "What is your dream, Al?"

"I don't know," Al replied.

"Well, if you could do anything and you knew you couldn't fail, what would it be?" I dug deeper.

"I'd love to skateboard, produce music and I also love filming and editing videos," Al replied.

"Then why don't you do one of those things?"

"Because there are too many people out there doing that, and it's too hard to get noticed," Al said.

"Do you think there aren't a lot of people serving food?" I asked.

"That's true," Al agreed.

"Look, it's not like I own a massive chain that serves thousands of people, but it doesn't matter how many people are doing it, because the small amount of people that order my meals are the reason I love what I do. Don't worry about what other people are doing or how many people are doing it, just start doing what you love," I encouraged.

"What about my job?" Al said hesitantly. "I need to be able to pay my bills."

"I'm not saying quit your job," I replied. "I'm saying start doing what you love on the side until you can make it your full-time job. My friend Bernard always says: *one small action towards your dream each day, is 365 actions a year— that's massive progress.*"

"That's actually really inspiring, Julia, you should be a motivational speaker or something," Al laughed.

"I plan to be something like that someday soon!" I replied with a smile.

"I actually believe that," Al affirmed.

Al is an extremely talented person; he was just lacking in self-confidence. Like so many of us, he had created limiting beliefs that dictated his behavior and ability to accomplish what he truly wanted.

Al and I started hanging out almost every day. He was very tech savvy and helped me build my online profile for Juu's Kitchen.

"Al, you'll never guess what happened!" I called one afternoon after work.

"What happened?"

"Have you heard of *Body & Soul* magazine?" I asked.

"Have I heard of it? It's like the biggest health magazine in Australia!" Al gasped.

"After they saw one of my posts on the Juu's Kitchen page, they contacted me and asked me to write an article!" I yelled excitedly.

"That's amazing! Well done!" Al cheered.

"Thanks to you for helping me set it up!" I said. "But I have to say, I am a bit worried about it…"

"Why? That's the most exciting news!"

"Well, they want to hear my transformation story and I don't know if I want to share some of that with the world," I said.

"Why? You have a great story!" Al encouraged.

"Maybe, but the lady said I have to give a before and after picture, too," I said nervously.

"So, you look great now, what are you worried about?"

"Al, I've never shared photos from when I was bigger. I can hardly look at them myself, and imagine how much all the people I know will judge me."

"Seriously, don't worry about them. If your story helps even one person like it's helped me, I'm sure it will all be worth it!"

Al was right. If I'm honest, I had not overcome the fears that were running through my mind. So I agreed to the article. I sent in the photos that made me insecure, and made final touches to the article the night before it was published.

With the click of one button, I submitted my article. There was no turning back now. I was petrified of what I could wake up to, and barely slept all night. Funnily enough, the outcome wasn't what I expected at all.

To my surprise, I woke up early to dozens of orders. Inquires from all over the country, even in areas that I couldn't service, flooded my inbox. But what made it all worth it, were the messages from people saying that my story inspired them. Other people were going through the same thing. I couldn't believe it; it was as if I still hadn't woken up from my dream.

In the coming days, many people I knew also read the article. Soon people from the gym asked to order my meals. Ron and the other trainers were very supportive, but I had a lot of respect for the owner, and I didn't want to do business behind her back in her gym. The environment she had created had played such a big role in many areas of my life where I now felt so accomplished; everyone at the gym was welcoming and supportive. And working out there was always a lot of fun. I decided I would approach her about doing a partnership.

One night after work, I came home and created the business plan that I would later pitch to the gym's owner. When I finally met her, I was so nervous and unsure of myself. This woman was extremely driven and successful. Just the opportunity to meet with her was a privilege.

She heard my proposal and, a few days later after trying and loving our meals, she agreed to help me promote Juu's Kitchen. This was a really incredible achievement for me; I was overwhelmed with joy that I would get to work side by side with the woman who had helped change my life. The gym's supportive and encouraging environment had played such an integral role in my transformation.

"Hey Al, I need your help, but I think you're going to love it!" I said.

"What is it?" he asked.

"You remember how I collaborated with the gym?"

"Yeah."

"Well, we want to do a promotional video and we would like to pay you to help me film and edit it if you like?"

"Yeah, for sure, I would love to do that!" Al agreed.

"Great, I can't wait for you to meet them all, everyone there is so positive and nice!" I said. "Who knows, maybe you'll even want to join! See you there next Saturday."

The day of the filming had arrived. We had arranged trainers, models and people from the gym who wanted to volunteer and take part in the video.

The day itself was extremely stressful; again, I had taken on more than I could handle. Running the event, organizing meals for people to taste and doing the workout session, I felt completely overwhelmed.

On top of this, I was coordinating with the chef and the kitchen staff, who were working on the real orders. My anxiety was going through the roof.

I didn't take a single moment to enjoy the incredible moment that we had created; I was stressing about everything, from camera shots and angles to speaking with volunteers and responding to delivery inquiries. Time flew by. Eventually we had enough footage and it was time to head to the kitchen, help package the food for delivery drivers, then finally go home and begin editing the video.

For two weeks straight, Al and I taught ourselves how to use Final Cut Pro for eight to twelve hours a day after work. Almost every morning, we would stay up editing the clips until 5 a.m., until we were both exhausted and snappy enough to call it a night.

Then finally we had the finished product.

"I love it so much! It's perfect. I know it was hard but can you believe we did this?" I yelled in excitement.

"You know, Julia, this whole thing you did is pretty amazing," Al replied.

"What are you talking about? You're the tech genius that worked all of this nonsense out!" I laughed. "If it wasn't for you, I wouldn't even know how to turn on the computer!"

"It's not just about the video…this whole thing," Al continued.

"What do you mean?"

"What I watched you do was absolutely incredible. This has never been your field, but somehow you coordinated a whole gym. You got the owners and trainers, customers and even models to volunteer and be a part of this whole thing *you* created," Al complimented. "I just have no idea how you managed to do all of that alone, and now I look at this awesome video, it just really proves that anyone can accomplish anything."

"Wow, Al, I never even thought about it that way," I replied, realizing that he was right. "It's crazy, because I have been so stressed out in all of this, I haven't really even taken a moment to enjoy this whole experience."

"I know, I've watched you. You really need to take a moment sometimes, to appreciate yourself for all that you're doing. You have come such a long way since the crazy little party girl I knew years ago," he laughed.

Al helped me realize that none of this would have any meaning if I didn't start to slow down and appreciate the beauty around me. There was no use in achieving anything if the experience didn't create great memories.

Starting this business was one of the first things that I had ever followed through with. It created the momentum I needed, and the invaluable lessons learned led to future endeavors.

Lessons

BUILD THE RIGHT HABITS, FAIL AND LEARN

Gaining a bit of momentum can ignite a power within you to achieve all things in life. Momentum brings action and it is important not to get too hung up on the outcomes—remember, enjoy the process.

So how do we build momentum? First, we need to celebrate the small progress that we make each day, week or month. This leads to big action in time.

Next, train your brain to truly believe that there is no such thing as "bad." These moments that we may choose to perceive as bad, are in actuality your opportunity to grow. They give us a reason to make changes and help us sift through what we want and don't want.

In these moments, be open-minded and wait on the lesson. Use these moments to create strong, positive change in your life. My first business started on complete accident, from a moment that I once considered to be "bad." Had I not put on weight, I may not have eaten healthier, in which I probably would have not learned to cook or find passion in helping others do the same.

TAKE CARE OF YOURSELF PHYSICALLY: MIND THE 3 F'S

The Physical area of life has three components. I call these "The 3 F's in Physical." These are food, feelings and fitness.

I'm not here to preach the perfect diet and full-blown workout obsessions (the opposite actually). But there is no denying that what you eat, and how much physical activity you incorporate into your life, has a direct impact on your physical and mental health. How you feel about these things is also important and often missed.

To have fulfillment in the Physical area of life, we need to create a routine and lifestyle that is sustainable, practical and one that we feel good about. What I'm saying is, if you don't like broccoli, don't eat it! But do eat other fresh produce you enjoy.

If you don't like cardio, don't do it! There's no need to run two hours on the treadmill if you hate it. Go play tennis, swim, lift weights or go for a walk instead.

Once you discover what you enjoy, make a habit out of it and build momentum. You'll reach a better outcome, as long as you progress and advance. Take it slow at the start and don't try to over do it. There is no use in starting a crazy, restrictive diet or spending seven days a week at the gym if you don't enjoy it—it simply is not sustainable and you will quit or, worse, probably put the weight back on.

Every success starts in the mind. Get how you *feel* about it right and the rest will follow. Remember, it has to be practical, sustainable and enjoyable for you!

Whenever you do a task, don't forget to measure how you feel after completing it, not before. And, if you don't feel like doing something that results in a good feeling (like going to the gym), do it anyway. Always measure how you feel *after*, not before.

EMBRACE THE STRUGGLE

Begin to notice the things that are all around you. When you focus on your surroundings, everything seems more vivid, as if it starts to shine in an altered light. The trees begin to look greener, the water is more alive and the breeze feels fresher. The scents around you become more precise and fragrant, more so than you may have ever noticed.

The struggle softens when we allow ourselves to be consumed by the experiences, not the outcomes.

Build an Appreciation Empire; because if you can't be happy with what you have now, adding more to your life won't change it. Whatever the situation, regardless of the conditions, learn to be grateful and find the things that you are happy about now—not "when this happens" or "if I had that."

When you do something you love that serves others, you'll be energized by their phenomenal responses. For me it happened through finding fulfilment in the physical area of life, which also gave me a much needed, healthy hit of confidence at that time.

Don't strive for perfection. There is no such thing. If you break your diet, enjoy the bloody slice of pizza! Don't beat yourself up about it, and just do better in the next moment. Getting this right in your mind is crucial—we cannot link food or exercise to punishment or reward.

Of course, there will still be hard days, but this will be the case no matter what you decide to do. When I have bad days, I try to understand why they are bad and what causes them to be bad. This helps me understand more clearly what a good day looks like. On bad days, I fail, learn and grow stronger. Which helps me sort through what I want and don't want. When I struggled at first in Juu's kitchen, I was motivated to keep going by the undeniable certainty that I was helping others solve the same problem I had—it was the greatest reward.

I started Juu's Kitchen accidentally, out of the desire to fix myself. But it turned out that I was never broken; I was simply learning to improve myself and take advantage of opportunities. Today, I have no doubt that everything was a necessary component of my journey.

Juu's Kitchen turned into so much more than a hobby of cooking, because of the previous skills and adventures that life had given me. And through presence and awareness, I acted on the opportunities when they presented themselves.

It was the ultimate reward for me to share my fresh, healthy gourmet meals with people who wanted to lose weight, feel happier and be healthier, because I know how hard it was at the start. It was very important to me to achieve this without limiting myself and others to strict, unenjoyable diets.

I believe life *should* feel incredible, and it *should* be joyful! It is our job to find what will make it that way for ourselves, and then share these lessons with others.

I say "yes" you can have it all! You just need to apply the elements that will make you successful. And you absolutely can still eat delicious food that compliments a busy lifestyle, controls your weight and doesn't break the budget, like eating out does. Being food conscious does not need to consume your life, because you can make eating healthy an enriching *way* of life.

Diary Entry

May 21st, 2018 – Denver, Colorado

TO THE MOUNTAINS PLEASE!

Some things in life you just need to go through and conquer completely by yourself.

Yesterday, I stood, full of gratitude and inspiration, on Mt. Evans in Denver. It was a clear feeling of being incredibly blessed at how I had come to live such a beautiful life. This world is so much more magnificent with each moment, especially in comparison to how I once used to feel.

Everything I had ever wanted and imagined have not only manifested, but the outcomes are better than I ever expected. It's an exhilarating game and the reward is worth the work. I had an amazing feeling of accomplishment yesterday.

I am here in Colorado this week for work, and I very much wanted to see the mountains. While this would only be a two-hour drive, the problem is, I'm still new here and haven't driven on the other side of the road before (we drive on the left in Australia). And I can't exactly get an Uber to "the mountains please."

Aside from my fear or driving (or crashing) in America, I am useless with direction and usually rely on a GPS to get anywhere. Of course, there was no reception out in the wilderness.

Pondering whether to go or not was unnerving. I had the car; the only thing stopping me was me. I'm grateful, however, that I have built up my physical strength to be able to do this. It would never have even been a thought, nor a possibility, a couple of short years ago.

I decided to do it, so after a whole day of searching, getting lost and nearly starving (because I'm unprepared like that), I finally stood on top of the mountain. The feeling of accomplishment rushed through me.

Fear and limiting beliefs could have stopped me from seeing this incredible sight; I am proud that I did not allow them. Standing literally on top of the world, I thought to myself, *"Were you really going to not see the mountains in Colorado, because you are scared to drive and believed you can't find the way?"*

When in life is it OK to let your fears and beliefs limit you? Never! At least try and give it your best shot.

You can do anything you want. Turn your "can'ts" into "cans" and your dreams into plans.

KEY POINTS:

1. What you eat and your physical activity has a direct impact on your health, overall well-being and fulfilment. Taking care of your body is critical. Don't ignore the Physical area of your life or any of the other seven areas.

2. Don't strive for perfection or get hung up on the outcomes. Find the activities and foods that bring you joy and make them habits. The outcomes will come.

3. Don't over do it. Create balance and don't beat yourself up if you screw up. Every moment is a chance to start again and get it right.

4. Most people in the gym, or any class or sport, are not judging you. Though even if they are, it's not your problem. Don't be afraid of getting out of your comfort zone.

5. Start building momentum, and measure how you feel after completing tasks or activities. If you don't feel like doing an activity that results in positive emotions, do it anyway!

ACTION STEPS:

1. Find one hour per day to do some form of physical exercise. This could be going to the gym, playing tennis, swimming or going for a walk.

2. Take a look at what you eat. Without any crazy diets or restrictions, find ways to substitute what you already eat with healthier options. For example, choose whole grain instead of white, replace meats and carbs with more veggies, or change one meal a day into a healthier one. For recipes and ideas, visit www.bestlifeing.com.

Chapter Eight

BROKE LIFE TO BEST LIFE

AREA OF LIFE 7/7: FINANCIAL

Bernard gave me a copy of his book *Flipping burgers to flipping millions*, a book about financial freedom, which wasn't a topic high on my values at that time. But I did enjoy the stories that he wrote. The book captured my imagination and it also introduced me to thinking about my "legacy"—a word I probably had to Google at the time.

After reading the book, I was inspired to start saving. And in the coming months, I did a good job of budgeting and putting aside a portion of my paycheck for my future and new craze focus I called "legacy." But in reality, the money that I saved would only be blown in a few months.

FRIENDSHIPS AND THE MEANING OF TRUE LOVE

I awoke to the sound of my phone ringing. David, a long-time friend from Miami, displayed on the screen. Throughout these years, he had introduced me to his group of close friends. But this isn't just an ordinary group of friends; they have something very rare and special about them. I had the pleasure of meeting them on my many McDonald's business trips to the

USA, which I would extend to spend extra time with these people. Initially, I did this just for a good time. I always experienced joy and inspiration when I spent time with these newfound friends; they were fun, kind and seemingly stress free. But one small moment was about to leave a permanent imprint on my perspective, and change the course of my experiences forever.

"I'm proposing to Christina in Greece next month. It's a surprise and the whole gang is going to be there!" David announced on the phone excitedly, inciting me to perform an efficient calculation of my finances.

"I'm there!" I yelled spontaneously, without consideration of any financial limitations.

The following month I stood on the streets of Mykonos. As our flights arrived staggered throughout the day, each of us were greeted at the 10 bedroom mansion, which was situated high on a mountain, overlooking the city lights, island and surrounding ocean. The overjoyed greeting I received upon arrival felt like pure love and brought with it a feeling of elation and excitement for the week ahead.

Soon there were 17 of us. Exhilaration flooded the kitchen area where we had all gathered. The ambiance echoed excitement, and we cheered and exchanged hugs with each person. Champagne bottles poured and celebration shot glasses clinked as we reunited from opposite sides of the world in this heavenly place.

No one in the group had a clue of how the proposal was to unfold, this included David, whose nerves were reaching their highpoint. Nobody wanted to ask him the details, fearing they would only cause him more pressure. Without the need for inquisition, we soon understood that our first sundown in Mykonos was about to become one of our most memorable sunsets ever. For his unexpecting girlfriend Christina, it would be the romantic fairytale story of a lifetime.

We had all agreed to dress in all white, and met on the marble stone balcony at the top of the mansion. Christina thought we were just going to watch the sunset together as we all cheerfully made our way up to the balcony.

David's nerves were becoming increasingly obvious as we toasted our glasses and stepped up onto the bricks that outlined the circular space. Slightly confused, Christina attempted to follow our lead, signaling David to come up, with a tug of his hand. She was met with his resistance. The brief interval between our synchronicity and her confusion, enlightened David that it was the perfect moment.

As he reached for his right pocket and bent on one knee, the world felt to have stopped for a second. I couldn't blink, in the fear that I would miss a moment of this magic. Her face lit up as she comprehended the situation. The confusion turned into a radiant smile as a tear of joy rolled down her cheek. She whispered, "yes," with a slow nod, humbled by his request. She kneeled down to meet him on the marble ground, embraced him in her arms and sealed the deal with a kiss. In a joyful cheer, we united our raised glasses.

This and many other moments, both during the week-long Mykonos trip and several prior trips to Miami, made me realize what love truly is. Not just the romantic type of love, but the love that these people displayed every single day: a love for life and one another, a love for kindness and joy, a love for gratitude and experiences, a love for presence and peace, a love for health and helping others. Their love was not conditional, and there was not a shortage to preserve. It was individually pure, unique to each person and welcomed abundantly. Together, their love was an enormous energy, a powerful force. Being consumed by their love wasn't difficult. And without resistance, I allowed myself to be filled by this deep, expansive force. I knew I would never forget this moment or the incredible feeling that it brought.

DIGGING OUT OF MY $30,000 DEBT

When I returned home to Sydney, Australia, I was ready to get back into routine and focus on my financial area of life, as well as my other goals. That year, which I referred to as "Broke Life," I was focused on getting out of more than $30,000 worth of debt (not including my car loan), which I had accumulated over the years from traveling, eating out, partying and buying the latest material possessions, clothes, bags, shoes, etc.

In order to achieve my goal of getting out of debt in 1 year, I had to live off less than 50% of my salary for the entire 365 days, a very difficult task for someone who had been living off almost double her yearly earnings for many years prior. After paying the rent and a small allowance for groceries and bills, I permitted myself to have approximately $70 AUD for luxury spending on things like eating out, drinking and new clothes. This was about $50 USD in 2016, which was extremely little for an entire week, repeated 52 times.

At that time, I hated Broke Life, to say the least. I felt ashamed and stupid, despised saying "no" and missing out on events, and couldn't stand the self control required to give up life's pleasures. Fortunately, working full-time and also running my business full-time consumed most of my hours and often took my attention away from the fun I couldn't take part in. Soon, instead of focusing on what I was missing out on, I began to see the cumulative effect of my small daily actions.

My meal prep business was booming, and I had created consistent healthy eating habits and a regular schedule at the gym. After one year, I was out of debt and I had even managed to build up a solid amount in my savings account. I felt fitter and stronger than ever before, both physically and mentally.

The year flew by. And after accomplishing so much in so little time, I realized that anything is possible. Nothing in this world causes my limitations except the power of my own mind.

On Christmas day of 2017, my friends and I were making plans for New Years Eve. The options were all the same and I could no longer justify spending hundreds of dollars for a nightclub entry fee, one of which was $700 just to walk in the door. Juu's Kitchen was closed for the holidays and I was on leave from my now part-time job.

The following day, I was on a flight to Miami to surprise my friends, whom I had missed immensely.

As always, I was welcomed with joy and excitement. The group had so much dynamic and their wonderful energy filled me with enthusiasm once again.

Bern and Lynn are a very successful couple who are always a bundle of joy to be around. Their success is not only career and financial, but in that they are fulfilled and present in everything they do. Bern and Lynn lead a life of gratitude and abundance regardless of any obstacles they may encounter. They teach me new things about life and the world, and they challenge and inspire me to achieve my goals. They truly believe in me, and back my decisions. But most importantly, they demonstrate the ultimate happiness, gratitude and satisfaction for everything they have, each and every day.

Christina and David are strong-minded and loving. They are natural romantics and they care about others. They are radiant and thoughtful, and they spread their magical energy to everyone they interact with. They showed me my first taste of what true love can look like: two people made perfectly for each other. Although my parents always displayed true love, I wasn't old enough to understand. David and Christina remind me of what I imagine my parents to have had. They welcomed me into their world, and blessed me with nothing but love, and sometimes even a bit of tough-love when I need it.

Christian and Marek are probably the two most appreciative and grateful people I know. No moment is taken for granted, and every experience they encounter is a moment to give thanks. They are full of love and support for each other and all of those who surround them. When we eat dinner together, Christian will always have us go around the table and share positive stories, grateful moments or positive affirmations. Christian and Marek publicly acknowledge their blessings and, with that, make us better, more appreciative people as well.

Migs and Frank are my partners in fun! They are always the last ones standing, willing and excited to show me this beautiful city. To this day they still challenge my opinions, prove me wrong when it's needed and give me great advice. They are honest and caring, stern but fair and they, too, celebrate success with me. We can have the world's biggest debates over a beer, and overall, they motivate me to be a better person.

These are some of the people who inspired me and showed me a way of life that I couldn't have even dreamed of. All of these people have taught me a true way of loving, giving and receiving. Find the people that make you better and cherish them by being an awesome person yourself.

My wonderful 10-day holiday in Miami for New Years was now over, and I was ready to come home to Sydney and start a fresh new year. This time, I felt excited to write my goals. I was sure I knew what I wanted and where I needed to focus my energy to achieve success.

BREAKING FREE FROM NORMAL

In my Sydney apartment, I sat down on my bed and began to write down my goals. My gym and health goals: lose X weight, lift X lbs. Then business growth goals: $X more sales, X new customers and X more social media followers. And lastly, work targets, based on my company's review of KPIs (key performance indicators).

Finished, I set down my pen and reviewed my list. At that moment, I realized that I didn't really want any of these things. They were just what I felt I was "supposed to" want.

"I can't imagine spending another whole year doing these things," I thought to myself. *"This is what I should want, but what is it that I truly desire deep inside?"*

I pondered a moment; between my job and juggling the meal prep business, I had completely burned myself out. And although Juu's Kitchen was an incredible experience and very much a needed part of my growth process, if I am honest, it was never really my dream. In fact, after a year, the only thing I enjoyed about Juu's Kitchen was that it helped people like me achieve their health goals. Once I had a few weekends of chopping 40+ pounds of green beans for 4 hours straight, my passion for cooking disappeared. It felt like a job.

This realization was the final thing I needed to really move forward—to really appreciate that life was too short not to chase a dream. And now that I was convinced that anything is possible, I began to dig deeper.

If I could achieve anything I could ever imagine, knowing that I couldn't fail, what would it be? Two long term dreams popped into my head almost immediately.

"I want to finish writing my book, and I want to live in Miami." My next thought was, "Are you normal?"

No, I wasn't normal. But thank goodness I no longer needed to associate myself with that label.

Realizing this, I saw how far I had come. In previous times and for many years, I would have let this and similar thoughts stop me, even paralyze me from moving forward with an idea. But not this time. There was no excuse and I believed that no matter what happened, I would make it and would be okay.

"Are you crazy?" people would say. "What will you do for work? How will you get a visa?"

These fears often floated around in my mind. But I did my best not to allow them or other people's limiting beliefs change my decision.

"I don't know," I would reply with a smile. "I'm sure I'll figure it out, and if I don't, what is the worst that can happen?"

That question is incredibly important: *what is the worst that can happen?* I could fail and then be forced to come home to Australia (not terrible), start again, get another nine-to-five or start another business. I might get stuck out there and run out of money. But is that really the worst? No, the (true) worst thing that could happen, is never knowing what could have been.

The biggest enemy of any dream, is fear of what might happen or not happen. Fear is just another thought. Scarier and more intense, yes, but still just a thought.

I made the decision, and three months later, it was almost time to go. Packing up the final pieces of my life was so surreal, especially when I noticed the amount of possessions that once held so much meaning to me, so much value! These things would now become either donations, rubbish or storage. My entire life's worth of material objects had to be prioritized into just two suitcases, a carry-on and a personal item.

Not many of these material objects had any meaning anymore. They no longer mattered. In fact, letting go of all the clutter was so liberating; and the knowledge that I wasn't attached to it anymore was complete freedom.

My final night in Sydney was bittersweet. I said my goodbyes to everything I had ever known to be normal, and from this moment there would be no comfort zone. I took my last mental images of experiences that brought me comfort for so many years, the people that would no longer be just a short drive away and places I cherished and had called "home" for so long. This was the end of the final chapter to the only book I had ever read or written. Now it was time for me to start anew.

Turns out, it was the best thing I ever did!

Upon moving to Miami, I had three months to figure out my visa. Marriage was not on the cards, as I wanted to marry for love like my Miami friends I so admired. Business investment wasn't an option either, as the investment was $1,000,000, which I didn't quite have at the time. Finding work was going to be hard, but it was my only option—hard equals possible, which works for me.

Unbelievably, within just a few weeks of being in Miami, I met an incredible woman who offered to hire me and sponsor my visa. She continued to give me work for over a year, teaching corporate classes on whatever topic she needed her 900+ employees to learn.

I would do research, develop the content and hold numerous classes on various topics, such as customer experience, leadership, mindset, motivation and emotional intelligence. I would get so much joy from seeing the students learn and make progress, not only in their jobs and positions, but also in their lives.

This led me to my next venture. I began to turn all of my workshops and class content into online learning. So I partnered up with my Miami friend Lynn, and we were able to create a successful business in something we are both passionate about—helping others overcome their own obstacles and limiting beliefs. This was by far the best, most exciting and useful thing I ever did for myself and others.

THE CONNECTION BETWEEN HAPPINESS AND FINANCIAL FULFILLMENT

Broke Life taught me to value money. Before this I was enslaved to the borrowed lifestyle, paying back interest before making any dent in the large amount I owed. My money habits stemmed deeper though—they came from the limiting beliefs of myself and others. These limiting beliefs caused me to derive my sense of self from what I owed, did and had. I allowed my possessions to be my entire identity—I didn't own them, they completely owned me.

In our society, every "thing" is so highly honored, but no "thing" truly matters. Life is about feeling abundance in what you have today. Life is so beautiful and I am so incredibly grateful that mine is now emptier of "things."

I remember back to when it didn't feel this way, and I try to think and remember why. The true reason is perspective. Every moment I have ever encountered has been a combination of what I have asked for, and the challenges needed to get me there. For example, there is no way I could write this book without having gone through the stories that are in it.

The difference today is I now appreciate these moments, and refuse to identify as the "victim," no matter the circumstances. When something undesirable happens, we still have the option to feel good or to not feel good. So, if it's out of your control and already happening, ride it out. Search for any feel good thoughts and moments, rather than paying attention to what you can't fix right now. Time heals all anyway.

Remove the belief that "things are happening *to* you," and replace it with "things are happening *for* you" instead. Force yourself to find the best in every situation, and that's Best Life-ing.

WHAT DOES "HAVING IT ALL" FEEL LIKE?

We will always want more. We are forever desiring creatures, and that is completely OK. Therefore, change is inevitable and challenge is necessary.

Think about it. If you ever reached a point in your life where you are completely content, then what else would you need?

Would you really give up the fun and excitement of getting there only to never want anything more again?

If I said to you, "Here, have all the money, holidays, experiences, relationships, jobs or dreams you'd like. You can have anything you can think of. Have all of it right now and that's it."

What's next? What could possibly be next once you have it all and have done it all? This is why we really have to realize that the fun is in the journey. Life isn't about checking off another item on your bucket list. It's about the journey you take to get there.

Recently, I met and became very good friends with a billionaire, who had it and had *done* it all. He was one of the most unfulfilled people I have met. He often said to me, "I've run out of things to do."

He had traveled the world, had everything he wanted (or had the means to get it), was involved in countless charities, started many successful businesses, attended big and small events of all types, played every sport, ticked off his entire bucket list and more. Now there was simply nothing that energized or excited him anymore.

Having it all does not necessarily equate to happiness or fulfilment, so stop putting off happiness and fulfilment. The time is never perfect; the only time is now. There is no need to wait until "this" happens or until you have "that." Gratitude can help you find happiness now.

Even when you are completely fulfilled, having everything you ever wanted, there will always be a need for further goals. You will always seek to adjust your life in at least one way. So get used to the feeling that this job is never finished, and start enjoying the fun of getting there, which is happening right now.

Begin by visualizing the life and the things you truly want. Then believe, without any doubt, that they are for you. With a little bit of work, new routines and habits, and consistency to create momentum, they will be yours.

HOW TO THINK ABOUT MONEY

Like it or not, creating fulfilment in the financial area of life will first require some savings. Think about it, why would anyone invest in you if you don't invest in yourself first?

Investing in yourself requires sacrifice and discipline. After all, you can't possibly be in the space you want to be (in any area) if you continue to act in a way that brings about an opposite result. Spend your money consciously. And remember, investing isn't all about money; it's also about where and how you spend your time. So think about what is most important to you and spend your time and money in that space more often. Being more conscious in the financial area of your life will help you build a comfortable cushion of savings, which makes life a lot easier than living paycheck to paycheck. Change the way you view money, and your financial situation will change.

I strongly urge you to save at least 10% of your paycheck. You can always increase this later, but start here to build the habit and gain some momentum. Aside from self-investment, anything can happen. The recent global pandemic (Covid-19) really proved most challenging for those who didn't have a comfortable amount of savings. Life is much easier when you don't have to stress about how you will pay your rent and afford food when something unexpected happens.

In a crisis, don't fall victim—be prepared. Start to save.

Your personal beliefs around money may need to change. As we saw earlier, if you have limiting beliefs around money, it will be much harder for you to obtain and keep it. Your dream can and likely will make you money, if you can find a way to serve others. The more people that can benefit from what you do, the more money will flow effortlessly towards you.

Don't quit your day job (just yet)! The job you do today is what makes you money right now. So learn to link your tedious job tasks to your future dream. This will create a deeper sense of enjoyment in your work today.

Accept the fact that we will always want more, and now is the time to enjoy the process of getting there.

LIVING WITH LESS TO FIND TRUE WEALTH

Create some minimalism and remove all of the clutter out of your life. This will give you space to figure out what actually matters to you, and you will be surprised how much crap you can find that you hardly even use.

This "stuff" takes up space in your life and in your mind. And aside from this, removing all of the useless crap in your life will make you more conscious of the things you value. In the future, you may reconsider wasting hard earned money on other crap. Instead, save and invest in yourself.

The last part to financial fulfilment, is to give back, without wanting any recognition for it. Giving makes you truly feel wealthy. And you don't have to give much. You can do something as simple as buying a sandwich for a homeless person or giving things away instead of throwing them away.

Recognize that there are plenty of people who live with much less than you. Do what you can to help and do it selflessly. We are all here to share this beautiful world; let's lift one another and help those in need.

We must give, to align ourselves to receive.

Diary Entry

May 29th, 2018 — Havana, Cuba

A TOURIST AND A LOCAL MAN

Another beautiful week in Miami has just passed, and I have now found myself in Havana, Cuba. It's crazy to realize that your thoughts *can* really become your reality. Cuba was never on my top list of places to go, nor have I had the urge to travel lately. But having a break is nice after all the effort it's taken to move to my dream city! Although I have been happy and content in Miami, something has been missing.

I had a deep feeling of having enough: I wrote in my gratitude diary every day and my Appreciation Empire was huge. Everything I ever wanted was real, here and happening right now. I couldn't think of anything that needed to be different. So how was it possible that something still felt like it was missing? And why did I end up in Cuba to find it?

When you have everything you ever wanted, you will need a deeper sense of gratitude. For example, in this instance, I began to feel lost and have a sense of "what's next?". I have the dream job, amazing friends, family, money, a beautiful apartment and lifestyle, and the time to do what I want....

The question became, *"How do I make sure this time is not wasted? How do I fully embrace and appreciate its perfection?"* I didn't. I still spent copious amounts of time stressing about what I wasn't doing—the workload, the traveling, the time I didn't have to spend with my friends, and the Instagram post that I couldn't word properly. Even *everything* wasn't enough! And that is when The Universe sent me to Cuba.

To appreciate my life, I had to allow for everything in it to temporarily disappear...and I mean all of it. There was no way to communicate with my friends and family in both Australia and Miami. My debit and credit cards weren't working, because, of course, I forgot to let my banks know, and they were blocked for fraud. So my money was mostly inaccessible. And because I couldn't call my banks overseas, I had a small amount of cash to survive on.

I couldn't access the work that needed to be done, because there was no internet and obviously no social media.

On this rainy week, the nice weather was gone, along with all the perks, like gym, sauna, spa and jacuzzi. Even good food was hard to find, so all I had left were my thoughts, a laptop and a good Cuban coffee. This turned out to be everything I needed.

On my first day in Cuba, I woke up feeling amazing. *"Can you believe you are waking up in Havana?"* I thought to myself. This felt so incredible.

Enjoying life requires having faith, and knowing that you are always precisely where you need to be, going through exactly what you need to. To get what you truly and most deeply desire, you need to experience difficult times while understanding their place and their benefit. These moments are the ones that teach you the lessons you'll need on the next leg of your journey, and help you filter through what you want and what you don't want.

This morning while sitting alone at breakfast without any phone or other technology, I observed the world. I looked around and saw the poverty and the life these people were forced to live.

Last night, my Airbnb owner explained how the Cuban government puts caps and restrictions on people's earnings. People who earn more than the cap (which is $10,000) have their bank account swept. The owner told of how most people here earn between $20-30 a MONTH! And survive off that. And this morning at breakfast I saw some of the poverty first hand.

I saw a man sitting on the street. He was normal looking, dressed casually and I wouldn't assume homeless, but he had sadness and pain in his eyes. He had what looked like a notepad, and was writing something while sitting on the wet ground.

I glanced over at him a few times and thought it was nice to see someone "old-school," writing in a proper book, but I didn't think too much of it. After almost 30 minutes, he stood up and walked over to the table next to me where three English-speaking tourists sat laughing, taking photos and enjoying their morning.

As he walked over he gently showed one of the tourist men the piece of paper he was using, and on it was not writing, but a drawing of this English man. He gently placed it on the table; I glanced over and saw that the picture was really beautiful, his expression of appreciation for this man through his artistic passion.

One of the tourists stopped laughing and, barely having looked at the photo, dismissed the Cuban man by saying, "No, no sorry," while waving his hand.

As the Cuban man walked away, my heart broke for him. The pain in his face was devastating.

Yes, he was doing it for money. No, the tourist man didn't ask for him to do it. But his look of lost hope in that moment was clear as he walked across the street and sat down on a chair. I wondered how many times a day that would happen to him.

The tourist man continued to laugh and enjoy his morning with his friends, taking no notice of what had just happened. It was sad to see.

I walked over on my way out, "Excuse me, can you speak English?" I asked.

"Yes, poquito," he replied (meaning "a little" in Spanish).

"I saw your drawing and I thought it was beautiful," I said. "I know it wasn't for me, but I would like to buy it please. How much?"

"I can draw one for you?" he offered.

"There's no need, and I am late for something," I pretended. "I like this one. How much is it?"

"Anything is good. Do you have five American dollars?"

I looked in my wallet to see my last six dollars, then handed him the five and shook his hand. I kept the last dollar in case I could find a way to call my bank.

He was extremely grateful and I watched his eyes fill up with tears. Before mine did also, I walked back to my hotel.

This story isn't about judging the tourists who rejected his offer. They had every right. But this moment sparked something within me, and the urge to help was irresistible. These tourist men had to do what they did so I could experience my lesson. I happened to be in the right place at the right time.

We never really know what someone is going through. But in some countries with widespread poverty, I don't even think we can imagine. So the next time you complain about not having Wi-Fi or feeling hungry from skipping breakfast, think about how much more you have than most people in Cuba or other third world countries. Money isn't everything—more people live on less than you. And if you take the time to watch and observe what is happening around you, you may get a glimpse of what someone else is going through, by momentarily shifting some focus off yourself.

Thank you Cuba, the tourists and this wonderful man for showing me what I was missing: without helping others, my life will never be enough.

KEY POINTS:

1. Value yourself and your money; this is going to take savings and sacrifice. Declutter to find what truly matters.

2. Find a way to serve others. The more people you help, the more money you will make.

3. Learn to link what you do today to your future dream.

4. Limiting beliefs around money stops you from earning more of it.

5. Help others for no reason.

ACTION STEPS:

1. Evaluate where you are financially and where you want to be—write this dollar amount down. The number can be as outrageous as you want, but you have to believe it is possible for you to achieve. The main reason people can't instantly win the lottery or get rich quickly, for example, is because they themselves do not believe it is possible. The number you choose has to be possible in your mind, because what you believe is exactly what will happen. You don't have to be realistic, you just have to truly believe it. The law of attraction doesn't take jokes well and can't be fooled; it accepts your thoughts exactly as they are.

2. Make a list of all of the things you dislike about your current job. Next to this list, write down how these tasks will help you once you achieve your dream; for example, the tasks may teach you something as simple as self-discipline, which is a critical skill. Even

your dream will become a job one day. It will definitely come with phone calls you don't want to make, meetings you don't want to attend or admin work that you are not passionate about. You will always have tasks you don't want to do.

3. Start saving 10% of your pay. If you don't invest in you, no one else will either.

Chapter Nine

EVERY PIECE OF
THE PUZZLE MATTERS

Your bad days, months or even years do not define you. Good and bad experiences happen to everyone, but they do not determine your success in life unless you allow them. Whether your life experience has been as messed up as mine or worse, how you interpret your past is just that: an interpretation, or your perspective.

A wise man once told me, *"The way we feel about anything that happens to us, can only be measured by our own level of 'shit.'"* And by "shit," the wise man meant discomfort, for lack of a better word.

One Tuesday afternoon, I was writing in a local, quiet bar and a regular customer walked in and sat next to me.

"Hey, Dexter," I greeted him.

"Hey, Julia, how are you?" he replied.

"How did you know it was me?"

"I can recognize that accent from a mile away. Besides, you're the only one ever tapping away on that laptop of yours!" he laughed.

"But we have only spoken once before," I said.

"You become more aware of things when you only have your hearing to rely on. Anyway, how was your day?"

"Eh, it hasn't been the best," I replied.

"Why, what happened? Tell me about it."

"I just had a rough day at work. I was teaching a class and we had a lot of technical issues, which made it very stressful, and I didn't have a backup plan. So it was just a bit of a mess. I could tell students weren't as engaged as they could have been and I just feel like I should have prepared better," I explained.

"That's OK, at least you've learned for next time," Dexter comforted.

"Yeah, anyway I don't need to relive it, just learn and move on. How was your day?" I changed the subject.

"Mine wasn't very good either."

"Why what happened?"

"Well, I was walking home from the grocery store, and a guy jumped me and robbed me. He took everything I had, my phone, wallet and even some of my groceries," Dexter said very calmly.

"Oh my goodness, Dexter, I'm so sorry!"

"Oh no, nothing to be sorry about. These things happen. At least I am safe, and now I know that I don't need to be afraid of something like that happening. I know I can survive it."

"I feel terrible!" I said, feeling intense heartbreak that something so horrible could happen to such a nice and wonderful person.

"Why do you feel that way?" Dexter asked, maintaining his calm tone of voice.

"Well, here I am telling you about my petty problems at work, while you're dealing with a real serious and dangerous event!" I said, my anger turning to embarrassment.

"No, Julia, let's go back a moment. Before I told you my story, how did your day *feel* to you? On a scale of 1 to 10? 10 being shit."

"Well it felt like 10 before...but..."

"No but! You felt a 10 on your level of shit," he interrupted. "I probably felt a 10, too, when my situation happened. A level 10 shit still feels the same 10 shit to the person experiencing it, as does a 1 or a 4 or a 7. *The way we feel about anything that happens to us, can only be measured by our own level of 'shit,'* the circumstance is irrelevant."

"OK," I hesitated as I pondered the depth of his words, realizing their truth.

"Our experiences acclimatize us to our life situation and teach us ways to deal with the circumstances we're given. Usually a person who goes through an awful experience doesn't even feel as bad about it as the people who observe and judge it do. Like me being blind for example, most people could never imagine living without sight. But I have accepted and adapted to it. I don't feel as bad for me as you obviously would."

YOUR SCARS CAN BE YOUR DOWNFALL OR NEW BEGINNING

When you truly analyze this powerful story, there are two main lessons. First, everybody experiences things differently. There is no right or wrong way to feel in any situation. Secondly, we get to choose how we *feel* about any experience, whether it be good or bad. When something happens to you, try to view it from another person's perspective.

Whatever the specific scenario, every 10 shit feeling to anybody feels like their own personal version of a 10. Which is why it's important for you to deal with the bad experience, respond to it and bring it down to a one. This is where it can be helpful for you to think about *how* every piece of the puzzle matters. In hard moments, I like to think about and create an imaginary story about how this particular "piece" could positively impact my life. This helps me bring it down to a one.

There were many moments in my life where I felt low and thought I wouldn't make it through. When my dad died, when I put on weight, the breakups, losing (who I called) friends and struggling with debt. In those moments, I didn't feel happy, powerful or inspired. I felt like crap. I felt like I had to use all my effort, perseverance and strength to get to the other side, and just fighting through the pain took all of my energy. Today, I am thankful for each of those moments, because they shaped my character, made me stronger both mentally and physically and led me to the exact place I am in right now.

Today, I am extremely blessed to be a coach, author, inspirational speaker and serial entrepreneur who is truly living and breathing the life of her dreams while traveling the world! I stopped wearing the high school dropout label that held me back; I created my own destiny. Your dreams are everything, and anything is possible—but only once you overcome your own limiting beliefs and the ones others have of you.

232

Don't ever give up on your dreams like so many others have—"giving up" is simply a belief that limits you.

You may have noticed that my diary entries throughout this book were written from many places around the world. These were all also written in the last 18 months prior to this book being published. Traveling the world was my personal dream and my version of Best Life-ing. To realize this dream, I first had to believe I could do it.

So the next time you experience a 10 shit feeling, think about how this piece of the puzzle may help you later on in life. Give this bad experience meaning and it will help you endure the pain and propel you toward your dream.

HOW THE 7 AREAS OF LIFE FIT INTO THE PUZZLE

Every piece of the puzzle matters. Each piece is uniquely cut, just like each situation in your life is unique. And these pieces (or experiences) build and shape you for something greater.

For your life puzzle to be complete, you will have to work towards the grander picture and not the individual piece. Once you create a big picture vision for your life by placing all those pieces in the right place, you are on the path to Best Life-ing. Because Best Life-ing is not conditional, it does not depend on circumstances or events. Instead, Best Life-ing is about having a deep fulfilment in the seven areas of life and knowing that, no matter the condition, you are going to be okay—you're just adding another puzzle piece to your life's big picture dream.

When my level of "miserable" was no longer bearable, I went "all in" on improving my life. I was sick of feeling like shit, being the victim and complaining about everything I didn't have. To be completely honest, I didn't even really believe I could break free from my negative habits.

When I started to search for myself, I expected to fail. To end up back where I started. But I figured I had nothing to lose.

What I didn't know back then, is that failure is strength, a call for adjustment and the road to revolution. Even if you completely fall apart, no matter what happens, you always can find a way to make it work—you have those survival skills.

Today, I look back and barely recognize the girl I used to be. But I remember her pain and isolation perfectly, hidden behind a compulsory smile that concealed my vulnerability. As each day, week, month or year finishes up, we need to reflect. Remember, it's appreciation for the simple, small things that can be life changing. Moments of pain provide clarity, and acceptance of everything drives the change. Believe. Because you and the moment are always already complete with everything you need.

Every moment is short and will be over in no time, so there is no moment worthy of stressing about. Be in it. Be present as often as possible; life is one big trip you don't want to miss.

If my family and I didn't go through the hardships that we did, if my dad didn't die when he did and if I wasn't bullied at school in my younger years, would I have developed a spiritual connection with my dad? Would I have been driven to leave a legacy in my dad's name? Would I have the same compassion for others, and would I want to dedicate my life to helping people rise above similar challenges? Believe me, none of this was easy in itself.

These experiences helped me build Spiritual connection.

Meeting every person that has ever entered my life was no accident either. Bernard, Simon and my friends in Miami, as well as Lisa and Dan were a hundred percent necessary to show me love, hurt, anger and bliss. Each revealed to me different contrasting paths I could take and helped me sift through what I want and what I don't want in my life. There may be pieces of the puzzle missing in your life. Understand that you cannot navigate through life alone and this is why we are built to have relationships. Every person is in your life for your positive growth and outcomes, even if that may be to show you a glimpse of your own reflection, or a picture of who you do not want to become. Seek guidance, ask questions and surround yourself with people who bring joy and growth into your life. There is no success without others—nobody is self-made.

These experiences constructed my Social area of life.

If I hadn't had enough of my drug and alcohol abuse, party-going lifestyle and bad decisions, would I have had the desire for any change? If I hadn't put on weight, would I have sorted out my health? And if I hadn't sorted out my health, would I have ever started a meal prep business? The answer to all of these is probably a "no."

These experiences contributed to my Physical well-being.

All the years working at McDonald's (which were so frowned upon) developed my work ethic. They gave me the skills to run my meal prep business and the confidence to get started. This inspired me to believe that anything is possible, which led me to seek personal growth. Starting a business forces you to learn, and it had a big impact on my book reading and research habits.

These experiences ignited a love for learning that fulfilled my Intellectual area of life.

If I hadn't applied the lessons I learned from Bernard and in books, Broke Life wouldn't have been successful. I probably wouldn't have gotten out of debt, and may have potentially racked up even more credit card bills. A better understanding and management of my money eventually led to my financial freedom. And believe me, even if I had accumulated the wealth back then, I would have found a way to spend it quicker.

These experiences produced my Financial freedom.

The lessons my family taught me were invaluable. They taught me that it is OK to be alone. None of my family members have ever been extremely tight or connected to me, in a way that other families are—and that is completely OK. I still love each of them with all of my heart, but I am fulfilled in the relationships that we have, and I do not feel alone. I know if I ever truly need them, they are there and love me also. Everyone is simply trying to do the best they can. Besides, having a close family doesn't magically make life better.

You may remember the diary entry from Chapter 2. The big family that I lived with in the USA still had the same drama and disagreements. They had many similar problems: child and teenage tantrums and household troubles that my small family had. They also had the same moments of love and bonding as mine did.

These experiences helped me accept my Relational area of life.

Terri once said to me that she knew I was made for bigger things. She was right, but I didn't believe her back then—because I didn't believe in myself. Nowadays, I often think about the trials that led me to where I am today. Every experience in my life, both good and bad, mattered. If even one piece of this puzzle was missing, would I be able to live the career and life that I have always dreamed of? Would I have ever made this move to the opposite side of the world? Would it be possible for you to be reading this book?

Working towards a greater purpose will help you keep your problems in perspective. Do not lose sight of your greater vision because of a failure, roadblock or even tragedy.

These experiences formed my Vocational area of life.

THROUGH THE PAIN, TEARS AND LOST FRIENDS, NEVER GIVE UP

Every piece of the puzzle matters, and there is a greater purpose to your life. To find your direction, you need to develop a vision and pursue it with complete faith. Don't get me wrong, doing this is not easy. I still deal with hard times and you will, too. But when you know that every piece of the puzzle matters, you will know *how* to deal: you search for answers and keep moving forward.

You may feel like a mixed-up jumble of pieces at times, overwhelmed with the many unknowns. Keep moving forward. You may feel that your life experiences have no connection and serve no purpose. This doesn't mean the big picture is gone; it means it's time to fit the pieces together.

Moving to Miami was my dream come true, but the minute the plane landed on the tarmac, a whole new world of difficulty became my reality. Everything unknown is difficult, and difficulty will always be there. But when I arrived in Miami, accepting and embracing that difficulty was crucial.

Starting a new life in another country wasn't easy. All of the basic things that I took for granted were no longer the norm. From getting a social security number, building credit, finding a place to live and furnishing it, to finding a job, getting a visa, running a business and starting a new business as well, my work was cut out for me. But deep down I knew that I had the power to make all of this happen. Following my dreams was no longer an "if I feel like it" or a "maybe I'll do that" option. My only choice was to succeed or go home back to Australia and start again.

Remember, anything you want will always be at the cost of something else—whether that be time, money, friends, work or location. To create change, you must pay some sort of price. The good news is, everything lost is lost deliberately and creates a path to your dreams. For the new improved version of yourself to be born, the old version of you must die. This process can be painful, as it was for me when I had to let go of Dan, Lisa and old habits that held me back. But you must believe with undeniable certainty, nothing will ever be lost. The experiences and people from your past will simply be your past.

Whether your path is long, confusing or repetitive matters not. It just matters that you don't give up. Instead, wholly embrace your journey. Release all expectations about what your path should look like. The right path for you is always in front of you. Keep searching for it, and you will inevitably one day complete your whole puzzle—so embrace your life as it is. Wouldn't it be better to be Best Life-ing now the rest of the way there?

When looking back on your journey, the feeling of fulfilment, satisfaction and pride you will experience is the ultimate reward. Knowing you did not give up, seeing what you are capable of achieving and following your heart will make it all worth it. Remember, life's joy is found in the exploration, not the destination. The victory is in the pursuit.

MY TOP 10 BEST LIFE-ING LESSONS

It's time to make Best Life-ing happen. For so long, I screwed around, wishing and hoping without any real vision, playing victim in my mind from self-inflicted situations. Throughout all the experiences, the lessons and challenges changed me. Here are the top 10 things I've learned:

1. It's all you – No one is going to spoon feed you your dreams or the lifestyle that you want. You need to go out and get it!

2. Begin today! – Start with what you have and where you are. One small action each day will make all the difference. Stop living in an imaginary future, or reliving and associating yourself with something that has already passed. Make it happen in the now.

3. Be your own sunshine – Love yourself first; if you don't love yourself to the highest degree, there is no way anyone else possibly could. And if you don't like something, you can simply take away its only power: your attention.

4. Forgive and spread love – Only you can control how someone can make you feel. Holding onto anger or other negative emotion is pointless because you are the only one who is feeling it. Actively look for opportunities to spread love instead; it's a much greater feeling.

5. Presence – The only moment we ever really have is now. Stop worrying about the future and/or letting the past define you. Create whatever change you want in the only moment you can ever truly do anything. The now.

6. Find your stillness – Take time to realign often. Everything on the outside can be managed from within. Stillness empowers you and helps bring clarity. This means a positive outcome is more likely to happen. Remember, the best outcome is always a positive one.

7. Screw what people think! – You'll never really know what's inside someone else's mind. Don't try to guess or analyze. Be your best, most incredible YOU. The only thoughts that matter are yours; besides, they're the only ones you'll truly ever hear.

8. Decisions – Always just do the next "right" thing you can do. Each experience is made specifically for your journey. Don't stress about messing up, you will anyway it's inevitable. Stop overthinking it, and make your decisions based on what you believe is the next right thing.

9. Work your butt off – Anything worth having takes work. Whether it's a relationship, career or personal goal, if you want it, it comes at the expense of hard work. Even once you obtain what you are seeking, keeping it requires more work.

10. Sacrifice – What you don't have will require the sacrifice of something you do have already. Where we spend our time and where we place our focus is where we are always most fulfilled. This means if we are not fulfilled in any area, we are simply not spending our time and energy there. Sacrificing and prolonging temporary indulgence will be a challenging part of Best Life-ing, but it is all so worth it in exchange for feeling truly fulfilled.

The actions needed for Best Life-ing may be an acquired taste, but they are the key to a life of true fulfillment. A life beyond your dreams today, and a version of you that is constantly evolving and flourishing through the adventures. Let the lessons and challenges change you to be brilliant.

ACTION STEPS:

Step one: Get clear on where you are right now, your ideal vision for all seven areas of life and your big reason to chase your dreams. Why do you want this for you? And why do you want it for others?

Get clear on what you want! See it and know that it is yours no matter what comes at you. Open your eyes to the opportunities already around you. Pay attention to everything that comes at you, and believe there is a purpose, for you have attracted it.

Step two: Do one thing a day to improve each of the seven areas of your life. Use your 168 hours a week wisely. Remember, one small action toward your goal each day is 365 actions a year. Plan and write down what your ideal day looks like. But whatever you do, don't stress when you don't *always* achieve it. Your plan is just your guideline—celebrate the wins. Here's an example of one of my ideal days:

6 a.m. – Wake up, meditate, practice gratitude

7 a.m. – Pray, eat breakfast and visualize (using the dream book)

8 a.m. – Work on business projects

11 a.m. – Write

2 p.m. – Gym and lunch

4 p.m. – Work on business or passion projects

7 p.m. – Social time/family time: cook dinner for family and friends or eat out. Make phone calls to overseas family and friends, or use social media to connect with friends.

9 p.m. – Read or relax and wind down

10:30 p.m. – Reflect on the day, practice gratitude and sleep by 11 p.m.

Your list may be completely different than mine. That's okay. The purpose of this exercise is to know what you want and strive for it.

241

Step three: Forget perfection. Execute as best you can. No, I don't perfectly live by the above schedule every day. Sometimes weeks or even months at a time can get messy and I can't seem to complete everything on my schedule. Different priorities pull us in different directions. But the clear vision of my ideal day makes it easier to follow and restart when I don't feel aligned. Write out the perfect day for you and try to live it as much as you can.

Celebrate the small wins like the Moore family, and don't punish yourself when you mess up or have other priorities. Get present. Be happy now. Use positive self-talk to recognize your accomplishments, instead of focusing on what you didn't complete. Celebrate everything.

Stay determined. Every "no" is a detour to a greater "yes." A "no" is not a letdown. I had 36 nos before my "yes" for a visa. I had 12 nos before a "yes" for my apartment. When wondering if it was possible to move to Miami, I told myself "no" countless times. For nearly 10 years, I made excuses, which were really just "nos" in disguise.

Remember the saying in Chapter 5? *Some will, some won't, who cares, who's next?*

Step four: Practice gratitude and review your progress as often as you can. This could be daily, weekly or a few times a week—just have the plan and try your best to stick to it. Go easy on yourself. Life is supposed to be fun, and the journey is supposed to be full of excitement.

Let's do a quick gratitude practice together. Say the below with me aloud.

I am grateful...for every moment that challenged me and made me stronger
I am grateful...for every "no" that lead to a better "yes"
I am grateful...for every mistake that became a lesson
I am grateful...for every heartbreak that made me seek a better tomorrow

I am grateful for every person from my past and the magic they brought into my life. I am grateful for all of the things and people that are part of my life today.

Step five: Stay focused on your mission. Don't let anything or anyone discourage you. Everything is either an opportunity, distraction or lesson—put it in the right place.

EMBRACE YOUR LIFE & SHARE YOUR LOVE

Ultimately, no matter where you are and what you are doing, it is *you* who decides if an experience will or will not work. Only *you* can choose if an experience is beautiful, regardless of the conditions. Loving all of life—every person, moment or challenge—whether good or bad, is unconditional love: unconditional love for life. And when you spread that magic, your world becomes magic.

Regardless of what challenges you face, or how bumpy the road may be, have faith that there is something better. This outlook will open doors and bring the many teachers, experiences and opportunities you need to transform your dream into a reality. Don't limit yourself.

I can't stress enough—love your journey, because one day even your dream becomes a job. Now is the time to appreciate all that you have and embrace wholeheartedly all that you are yet to receive.

I wish you so much love and abundance, my beautiful reader. I wish you laughter and that your many dreams become reality. I hope that you choose to add the "-ing' into your version of Best Life. And I wish you many blessings, endless enthusiasm and deep peace.

Share your success stories with me and the world—because we are the authors and editors of our stories, the teachers and artists of our destiny. You have the power to bring magic into your experience and the lives of others. You can shape the future. And you are the inspiration, imagination and the magic behind your dreams.

ACKNOWLEDGEMENTS

Firstly, I want to say thank you to all of the people. The ones who have taught me, inspired me and have written or recommended books. The people who helped me up when I was down, kicked my butt when I needed it and showed me what I do and don't want out of life.

Bernard, thank you for always having time for me. You are an amazing mentor, friend and just overall an incredible human. You have taught me so much, and without you I would probably still be an angry little girl who didn't know how to dream and didn't believe in herself. Thank you for always pushing me to be better and showing me the importance of helping others. Thank you for inspiring my confidence, putting everything into perspective and all of the endless hours you have spent teaching me, counselling and pushing me to be my best self.

Mum, you are the most amazing woman in the world to me. Thank you for teaching me strength, kindness and love. Thank you for always doing your best and showing Nat and I everything we know. You are the strongest woman I have ever seen. Thank you for working so hard to give us a wonderful life, thank you for loving us, worrying, putting us first and doing so much to give us a head start. I miss you, I love you and I want you to move to Miami with me!

John, by far the best editor I could have ever imagined working with. Thank you for holding my hand throughout the whole process. Your honest feedback, attention to detail, patience, advice and exceptional writing skills have made this journey so enjoyable, and without you there is no way this book would be as awesome as I think it is! I am so glad I found you, you have always been a blessing and bundle of joy, and I totally think of you as a mate now. Your emails excite me and I look forward to all of our future projects, and working together for a long, long time!

PJ & Mez, my dream team! Thank you for your creative magic. You guys always bring so much life and vibrance to my messy ideas. Thank you for a wonderful decade-long friendship, mostly our deep exploring conversations, endless laughs and crazy adventures. Thank you, guys, for being solid, genuine, honest and strong. You are inspiring and kind, and you have always supported me and cheered for my success, as I will always do for you also. Thank you for the early JK days, PJ for making it operationally possible and Mez for helping me spread the word, and being a loyal customer! You guys bring me joy, I miss you heaps and your drive and accomplishments always inspire me and make me so much better. Always endless love for you guys!

The Moore & Jenkins family, my New York family! You guys have shown me so much love from the very first moment I met you. Thank you for bringing me into your world, making me feel like family and exhibiting love, confidence and the most phenomenal energy. You are all so talented, enthusiastic and venturous. You have taught me to celebrate everything, as well as appreciation and love on a whole new level. Your triumphs brighten up my life, and the tremendous radiance you bring to everyone's life you touch is simply remarkable.

Krystle, thank you for being such an awesome woman and extraordinary friend. You are such a powerful, secure and independent woman, and a truly incredible friend and mother—Pariss is one lucky little princess, and I'm grateful to call you bestie! Thank you for the new adventures we have shared, the laughs, the tears and the world of magic we have experienced together. You make me brave, more ambitious and your drive to succeed is truly electrifying! Thank you for taking the time to listen to my book start to finish, and all of the helpful feedback that turned it into what it is today. Love you to bits and cheers to our fun and exciting future together.

Omid, I always say I hit the jackpot with you! You are a total genius, so well composed and you always know what to do. You have been nothing short of a blessing. I love our deep debates about science vs the universe, I love your simple and logical approach to everything and how you are always able to get a positive outcome in any situation. You have the whole world ahead of you, and I know you are going to kill it out there and I can't wait to watch and be a part of it. Thank you for our nightly reading sessions in the early days, your super helpful feedback, honestly and endless love and support! You are amazing, and here it is in writing: one day I'm gonna buy you that boat ;)

My amazing day one Miami mates: David, Christina, Bern, Lynn, Marek, Christian, Migs, Frank & Stevo. Where do I start? You guys are everything! You guys are the friends who really are my family and I am truly grateful every single day to have such an amazing group of people in my life. You have always inspired me with your happiness, gratitude, intelligence and overall uplifting way of life.

Thank you, DC, for your kindness and not only giving, but teaching me the meaning of unconditional love. None of this would be even imaginable without you. Thank you from the bottom of my heart.

Thank you, Taylors, for demonstrating the first perfect marriage I have ever seen. You guys are genuinely the most grateful people I have ever met and you always remind us to never take the precious moments we share for granted.

BerLynn, thank you for your always chill, drama-free, warm-hearted way of life. Thank you for the fun memories we continue to create, your limitless optimism in my success and the confidence you have in doing business so we can change the world together. Bern, you are one of a kind, and I have always strived to be half the bright, beautiful and sophisticated woman you are, and, Lynn, your wisdom is infinite and you are the best business partner ever!

Migs, thank you for giving me my first start in this wonderful country, thank you for sparking the inspiration to make this massive move and teaching me so much about adulting out here. Thank you for all of the amazing times we have shared together, the wonderful conversations and especially our exciting adventures on 'framily' holidays. Thanks for always making so much effort to show me all the wonderful things this beautiful world has to offer, and going above and beyond to be a great friend.

Last but most definitely not least, Frankie, Stevo & Rudy! You guys are the best. Like brothers, you always look out for me, give me amazing advice and are always ready to laugh and spread joy and love. I love all of your ideals and values, and your authentic desire to bring high-spirits and light-heartedness to those around you. Thank you for all of the wonderful times we spend together, beautiful sunsets, meaningful conversations, and Frankie mate—thanks for teaching me how to finally ride a bike!

ABOUT THE AUTHOR

Speaker. Author. Entrepreneur. Julia Brodska is the owner of two successful businesses and regularly presents her Best Life-ing principles to audiences large and small as she travels the world. She is the living embodiment of a woman who lives her dream life. But it wasn't always this way.

Julia was once overweight, buried in $30,000 of debt and filled with self-doubt. Mentors and positive role models helped turn her life around, and she documents this transformation in her first book Best Life-ing. Julia's mission is to do for you, what her teachers did for her—to inspire, instill confidence and provide a path to your dream life. Today, she helps young adults and corporate clients do just that.

Her meal prep business, Juu's Kitchen, helps customers get healthy and lose weight using a gourmet meal prep plan that, when combined with exercise, helped her lose 30 pounds in one year. Her company Best Life-ing focuses on holistic health and wellness coaching, and her company Brosell Business Solutions teaches corporate employees how to achieve more in life and work, following her Best Life-ing framework.

When Julia isn't running her businesses, you can find her practicing yoga or meditation, rollerblading or getting her sweat on at the gym, usually every day.

To book Julia for a speaking engagement, get in touch with her at **julia@bestlifeing.com**. And to learn how to save time, lose weight and get healthy, cooking delicious gourmet meals, sign up for her newsletter at **www.bestlifeing.com**.

BEST
Life-ing

Are you feeling stuck in life? Our online courses are for anyone who has unsuccessfully attempted to improve their overall health. It is designed so that you can go at your own pace. With a team of 20+ healers, teachers, and coaches, Best Life-ing can help you to achieve your dreams and fireach fulfilment in the 7 Areas of Life.

Reach out at www.bestlifeing.com, call us at (727) 777-LIFE, or contact Julia directly at julia@bestlifeing.com!

CAN YOU PAWWWWWLEASE LEAVE A REVIEW?

Cute puppy photos aside, let me be real for a minute.

We're both Amazon shoppers, and we both know that legitimate reviews are incredibly helpful when buying a product.

And as an independent author, reviews are critical. So can you pawwwlease, ahem, please help out and write a review?

I'm not asking for an epic 4 paragraph review (we're all busy), but just a few sentences would be helpful. 1 star, 5 stars or anywhere in between is cool! Regardless, thanks for reading this book, and I appreciate your time.

END NOTES

INTRODUCTION:

1. "Definition of best adjective from the Oxford Advanced American Dictionary." *Oxford Learner's Dictionary*, Oxford University Press, 2020, www.oxfordlearnersdictionaries.com/us/definition/english/best_1 (accessed 3 July, 2020).

2. "Definition of life noun from the Oxford Advanced American Dictionary." *Oxford Learner's Dictionary*, Oxford University Press, 2020, www.oxfordlearnersdictionaries.com/us/definition/american_engli sh/life (accessed 3 July, 2020).

3. "Definition of -ing suffix from the Oxford Advanced American Dictionary." *Oxford Learner's Dictionary*, Oxford University Press, 2020, www.oxfordlearnersdictionaries.com/us/definition/american_engli sh/ing (accessed 3 July, 2020).

CHAPTER ONE:

1. "Revolutions of 1989." *Wikipedia,* 28 Jun. 2020, en.wikipedia.org/wiki/Revolutions_of_1989 (accessed 3 July, 2020).

2. MacGill, Marcus. "Dementia: Symptoms, stages, and types." *Medical News Today,* 1 Dec. 2017, www.medicalnewstoday.com/articles/142214 (accessed 3 July, 2020).

3. "Definition of belief noun from the Oxford Advanced American Dictionary." *Oxford Learner's Dictionary*, Oxford University Press, 2020, www.oxfordlearnersdictionaries.com/us/definition/american_engli sh/belief (accessed 3 July, 2020).

4. Kelly, Matthew. *Perfectly Yourself 2nd ed.* BookBaby, 2015.

CHAPTER TWO:

1. "Marijuana DrugFacts." *National Institute of Drug Abuse*, 25 Jun. 2020, www.drugabuse.gov/publications/drugfacts/marijuana (accessed 3 July, 2020).

2. "Abraham: The Law of Attraction." YouTube, uploaded by Abraham-Hicks Publications, 8 Feb. 2008, www.youtube.com/watch?v=sb749f30Z8w&list=PLnmFl-NoZ0wp7XeB9oIFxWaWmX261I2_j&index=4 (accessed 3 July, 2020).

3. Demartini, John. "How perceptions affect our health." Demartini Institute, 2020, www.drdemartini.com/perceptions-affect-our-health/ (accessed 3 July, 2020).

4. "Being present in relationships." YouTube, uploaded by Eckhart Tolle, 4 Feb. 2008, www.youtube.com/watch?v=vshBnR4Z9x8 (accessed 3 July, 2020).

5. Levine, Amir and Heller, Rachel. *Attached: The New Science of Adult Attachment and How It Can Help You Find - and Keep – Love.* TarcherPerigee, 2012.

CHAPTER THREE:

1. Maxwell, John C. *The 5 Levels of Leadership: Proven Steps to Maximize Your Potential.* Center Street, 2013.

2. Godman, Heidi. "Regular exercise changes the brain to improve memory, thinking skills." Harvard Health Publishing, Harvard Medical School, 9 Apr. 2014, https://www.health.harvard.edu/blog/regular-exercise-changes-brain-improve-memory-thinking-skills-201404097110 (accessed 2 July, 2020).

3. Pratim, Partha. "Good Reakers Make Good Leaders." *TEDxTheNewtownSchool,* TED, 24 May, 2018, www.ted.com/talks/partha_pratim_das_good_readers_make_good_leaders/up-next (accessed 3 July, 2020).

4. Sharma, Robin. *The Monk Who Sold His Ferrari: A Fable About Fulfilling Your Dreams & Reaching Your Destiny.* Harper San Francisco, 1999.

5. Tolle, Eckhart. *The Power of Now: A Guide to Spiritual Enlightenment.* New World Library, 2004.

6. "Abraham-Hicks Process for Meditation." *The Law of Attraction Resource Guide*, 2020, www.lawofattractionresourceguide.com/abraham-hicks-process-for-meditation/ (accessed 3 July, 2020).

7. Smith, Melinda; Robinson, Lawrence and Segal Jeanne. "Help Guide. Coping with Grief & Loss." *HelpGuide*, 1 Nov. 2019, www.helpguide.org/articles/grief/coping-with-grief-and-loss.htm (accessed 3 July, 2020).

8. "7 stages of grief." *ThriveTalk*, 22 Mar. 2020, www.thrivetalk.com/7-stages-of-grief/ (accessed 3 July, 2020).

9. Bronstad, Debbra. "The 7 stages of Grief Model." *Stages of Grief Recovery*, 2020, www.stages-of-grief-recovery.com/7-stages-of-grief.html (accessed 3 July, 2020).

10. Tolle, Eckhart. *The Power of Now: A Guide to Spiritual Enlightenment.* New World Library, 2004.

CHAPTER FOUR:

1. Kelly, Matthew. *Resisting Happiness: 2nd ed.* Beacon Publishing, 2016.

2. "Jump." YouTube, uploaded by The Official Steve Harvey, 10 May, 2019, www.youtube.com/watch?v=y-952IaLtKM (accessed 3 July, 2020).

3. Harvey, Steve. *Jump: Take the Leap of Faith to Achieve Your Life of Abundance.* Amistad, 2016.

4. Tolle, Eckhart. *The Power of Now: A Guide to Spiritual Enlightenment.* New World Library, 2004.

5. Jordan, Montell. *Becoming Unfamous.* NewType Publishing, 2017.

CHAPTER FIVE:

1. Kelly, Matthew. *Perfectly Yourself.* Blue Sparrow, 2017.

2. Knight, Sarah. *The Life-Changing Magic of Not Giving a F**k.* Quercus, 2015.

3. Murphey, Joseph. *The Power of Your Subconscious Mind.* Martino Publishing, 2011.

4. Ferris, Timothy. *The 4-Hour Workweek: Escape 9-5, Live Anywhere, and Join the New Rich: 2nd ed.* Vermillion, 2011.

CHAPTER SIX:

1. Roberts, Gregory David. *Shantaram*. St. Martin's Griffin, 2005.

2. Hicks, Esther and Hicks, Jerry. *The Law of Attraction: The Basics of the Teachings of Abraham*. Hay House Inc., 2006.

3. Boothman, Nicholas. *How to Make People Like You in 90 Seconds or Less*. Workman Publishing Company, 2008.

4. Groth, Aimee. "You are the average of the 5 people you spend the most time with." *Business Insider*, 24 Jul. 2012, www.businessinsider.com/jim-rohn-youre-the-average-of-the-five-people-you-spend-the-most-time-with-2012-7 (accessed 3 July, 2020).

CHAPTER SEVEN:

1. Camworth, Sam. *Storyshowing: How to Stand Out from the Storytellers*. Wiley, 2017.

2. Baker, Tommy. "44 Undeniable Ways to Build Momentum, Get Off The Sidelines and 10X Your Results." Resist Average Academy, 21 Apr. 2019, www.resistaverageacademy.com/44-undeniable-ways-to-build-momentum/ (accessed 3 July, 2020).

3. Davis, Charles Patrick. "Health tips for healthy living." *Medicine Net*, 2020, www.medicinenet.com/healthy_living/article.htm (accessed 3 July, 2020).

4. Blanchard, Kenneth and Bowles, Sheldon. *Raving Fans: A Revolutionary Approach to Customer Service: 2nd ed.* Harper, 2011.

CHAPTER EIGHT:

1. Kelly, Bernard. *Flipping Burgers to Flipping Millions: A Guide to Financial Freedom Whether You Have Your Dream Job, Own Your Own Business, or Just Started Your First Job.* Hyperion, 2011.

2. "Abraham Hicks - Manifesting Money 100k Fast." YouTube, uploaded by NinjaRockNRoll, 1 Oct. 2017, www.youtube.com/watch?v=Nt7q182As1o (accessed 3 July, 2020).

3. Abraham Hicks - Money is knocking on your door, let it in!" YouTube, uploaded by Abraham Fan, 1 May, 2011, www.youtube.com/watch?v=zM2PX4D092w (accessed 3 July, 2020).

4. Hill, Napoleon. Think and *Grow Rich: Rev. ed.* TarcherPerigee, 2005.

Made in the USA
Columbia, SC
11 May 2022

60249814R00164